D0210156

PRAISE!
A Matter of Life and Breath

PRAISE!
A Matter of Life and Breath

by
Ronald Barclay Allen

Ronald Barclay Allen

Psalm 146:2

THOMAS NELSON PUBLISHERS
Nashville

Library of Congress Cataloging in Publication Data

Allen, Ronald Barclay.
  Praise! A matter of life and breath.

  Bibliography: p. 245.
  1. Bible. O.T. Psalms—Criticism, interpretation, etc. 2. Praise of God. I. Title.
BS1430.2.A35   223'.206   80-23894
ISBN 0-8407-5733-6

Dedication

To the loving memory of the late

Reverend Theodore B. Hax,
1904–1965

Beloved instructor at the California Lutheran Bible School, Los Angeles, who taught me well the delight of the Old Testament and the joy of the praise of God. I shall not forget his exulting with the sons of Korah:

> As the hart panteth after the water brooks,
> So panteth my soul after Thee, O God.
> —Psalm 42:1 KJV

Contents

Foreword

It is my conviction that evangelical Christianity has suffered greatly because of its antipathy toward the past. Its anti-historical stance has cut it off from the great treasures of the church. This has been true in the area of theology, pastoral care, hermeneutics, and worship.

This situation, however, is being slowly reversed. There are a number of evangelical scholars, pastors, church leaders, and laymen who are reaching into the depository from the past to fill the current vacuum among evangelical Christians. I welcome *Praise! A Matter of Life and Breath* as one more indication of a maturing evangelical faith.

For this reason I am particularly pleased with Ronald Allen's suggestion that we rediscover the Psalms for worship. Worship is the weakest area of evangelical Christianity. We are strongest in the areas of evangelism, teaching, and fellowship. We are improving greatly in the area of servant-hood (application of the gospel to social needs) and the ministry of healing (counseling and care for the emotional needs of people). But depth in the area of worship is badly lacking. We hardly know where to begin, because we have lost nearly all contact with the past.

Our current experimentation in the area of worship is too reliant on the fads of the present. Contemporary popular verse and music is entirely too man-centered. The focus of much contemporary Christian worship is almost entirely on man and his needs, with no hint that God wants us to praise Him. Yet from proper praise our needs will fall into their proper places—and be taken care of.

This is why Dr. Allen's work is so important to the evangelical church. He wants us to recover the central form of praising God—the Psalms. Here is the heart of praise for the Old Testament people of God, the early church, and the Reformers. Here is the central source for the revitalizing of evangelical worship—both personal and corporate.

I hope this work will be read widely and taken seriously. I commend it heartily to evangelicals everywhere and pray it may contribute to the renewal of worship—a renewal sorely needed and basic to the life of the Christian community.

Dr. Robert Webber
Professor of Theology
Wheaton College

Preface

With apologies to the sloganeers of a worthy public relations campaign for good health, I wish to stress the pulsebeat of the Book of Psalms to be that *Praise Is a Matter of Life and Breath.* Praise is a matter of life! It is to be done by the living; it is not forthcoming from the dead (see, e.g., Ps. 6:5). Praise is a matter of breath! The last words of the Book of Psalms, in glorious orchestral accompaniment, shout jubilantly:

> Let everything that has breath praise the Lord!
> Hallelujah!
> (Ps. 150:6)

Not only is praise commanded of the living, but it itself is a measure of spiritual vitality. Those who are alive in the Lord, and who know they draw their very breath by His grace, delight to praise His name. Praise, then, is not only commanded of those with life and breath, but is a sign of life and breath in Him. It is also a tonic that keeps life and breath fresh in His service.

One writer on the Book of Psalms who has influenced me greatly is Claus Westermann. He is a German scholar who learned the praise of God while in a German prison camp during World War II. At the conclusion of his book, *The Praise of God in the Psalms,* he writes:

> ... *only* there, where death is, is there no praise. Where there is life, there is praise.

The possibility that there could also be life in which there was no praise, life that did *not* praise God, does not enter the picture here. As death is characterized in that there is no longer any praise there, so praise belongs to life. The conclusion is not expressed in the Old Testament, but it must still have been drawn. *There cannot be such a thing as true life without praise* [emphasis added].[1]

Yet, what is praise? Is it merely the repetition of a few catch-phrases, like a "Protestant rosary," in dull and lackluster liturgy? Is it simply the mindless clichés of bumpersticker slogans echoed by the remnants of the Jesus people movement? Surely praise is more than mumbling "Praise the Lord" or the ill-timed shoutings of "Hallelujah!" Even singing "Let's Just Praise the Lord!" does not really explain what praising the Lord truly is.

It is the purpose of this book to bring the current excitement about praise to its *source book,* the Psalms. For it is in the hymnbook of the Old Testament that we learn what praise is. Much scholarly activity has been expended in the last few decades on Psalms research. Some of this research is displayed in fine commentaries and technical papers that have appeared in learned journals. While many recent devotional books on the Book of Psalms have been written, few books have been addressed to the Christian public that stress the concept of praise from an exegetical foundation.

It is a secondary purpose of this book to express the issue of praise in the manner of *warm* scholarship. I have written from the standpoint of exegetical studies (that is, a detailed study of the original text), but to a much wider audience than most such studies appeal to. Some technical terms are used (with explanations) to keep the discussion precise. I am hopeful that the abundant use of illustrative material will keep the technical data in bounds.

This book, then, attempts to lead the reader back to the

[1]Claus Westermann, *The Praise of God in the Psalms,* trans. Keith R. Crim (Richmond, Va.: John Knox, 1965), p. 159.

Psalms, and then through the Psalms to the praise of the living God. The book is at times quite personal. No apology is made for this; I know of no impersonal way to express praise to God!

There is a fairly involved history to the makings of this book. Some of the materials were given as lectures at Southwestern Bible College, Phoenix, Arizona, as part of the Staley Distinguished Christian Scholar Series. I gave lectures on the Book of Psalms in slightly different formats at the Alaska Bible College, Glenallen, Alaska, and at the Asian Theological Seminary, Quezon City, Metro Manila, Philippines. Some of the Psalms presented (along with a good many other Psalms) were the text for sermons in churches and at Bible conferences throughout the western United States over the last several years. I owe gratitude to my ever-friendly mentor, Professor Bruce K. Waltke, Th.D., Ph.D., now of Regent College, Vancouver, British Columbia. I also owe gratitude (*utang no loob,* as it is said in Manila) to Western Conservative Baptist Seminary for granting me a sabbatical leave in Asia that allowed, among other things, the completion of this book.

Finally, a word should be given about the translations used in this book. Most of the English readings of the hymnic texts are my own and are characterized by the freedom of employment of the divine names *Yah* and *Yahweh,* where the Hebrew text so indicates. I have written elsewhere on the significance of the divine name.[2] In other cases the translation is noted by common abbreviations, such as KJV (the King James/Authorized Version, 1611), NASB (the New American Standard Bible), and NIV (the New International Version). Where words in translations are italicized it will be apparent from the context that the emphasis is mine.

A study of the Book of Psalms leads finally to a renewed commitment to our own hymnody. I find the fourth stanza of

[2]"What Is in a Name?" in William F. Kerr, ed., *God: What Is He Like?* (Wheaton, Ill.: Tyndale, 1977).

Joachim Neander's well-loved hymn, "Praise Ye the Lord, the Almighty," to be a splendid summary of the direction of this book:

> Praise ye the Lord!
> O let all that is in me adore Him!
> All that hath *life and breath*
> come now with praises before Him!
> Let the Amen
> Sound from His people again:
> Gladly for Aye we adore Him.

All Souls' Day, 1978
Quezon City
Metro Manila,
The Philippines

PART ONE

Getting to Know the Psalms

CHAPTER 1

The Psalms:
A Universal Favorite

Only a Philistine could fail to love the Psalms. Of all the books in the Old Testament, the Book of Psalms is the one most loved by the family of God. Within the Psalms we find expression to our deepest thoughts of reverence for God, our most excited joy in knowing Him, and our darkest terror in those moments we feel cut off from Him. In the Psalms we have it all: music, wisdom, beauty, truth, theology, experience, emotion, and expression. In the Psalms we have the Lord Jesus in bold prophecy and in subtle types. Most of all, in the Psalms we have the praise of God.

Not all of us love the Psalms in the same way or to the same degree. Some turn to the Psalms in moments of devotion or distress, but not when they are engaged in an exercise in Bible study. Pastors often read from the Psalms as a part of the congregational worship, but more rarely turn to the Psalms for texts for their sermons.

Once when I was asked to preach a series of messages to a rural congregation, I sent word that I would like to present several sermons on the Book of Psalms. It was not until some months later that I was told that this announcement had caused some concern at the time among the members of the pulpit committee. Some wondered if my telephone call had been received accurately. Perhaps, it was thought, I was going to *refer* to the Book of Psalms in my sermons. When it was understood that I was intending to *preach* from the Psalms, and that not one message, but a series of sermons was planned, the concern of the committee grew. Preaching from the Old Testament is rare, and preaching from the Psalms seems to be a genuine novelty. Finally, they decided to let the series proceed.

Whereas it may be true that lamentably few preachers develop exegetical sermons from the Psalms, this does not mean that God's people generally have ignored the hymns of Israel. Quite to the contrary—the Psalms are the most treasured part of Israel's literary gifts to the church. No part of the Old Testament is easier to approach for the Christian reader than the Psalter.

COMFORT AND CONFIDENCE

The Psalms have meant many things to many people through the ages. These lyrics have been of inestimable comfort to the bereaved. How very many times, for example, must Psalm 23 have been recited in funeral settings! Now chanted, now recited by rote; sometimes read with fervor, other times haltingly, with tears blurring the words—the Psalm of the Shepherd will never lose its luster. Who can ignore these words?

> The LORD is my shepherd;
> I shall not want (Ps. 23:1 KJV).

This Psalm of childlike confidence in God is rightly considered to be one of the finest in the Psalter. The many settings of this Psalm to music for the church attest to its continuing power and beauty.

Or hear again the opening verses of Psalm 91:

He that dwelleth in the secret place of the Most High
shall abide under the shadow of the Almighty.
I will say of the LORD,

18

He is my refuge and my fortress,
my God: in him will I trust (vv. 1,2 KJV).

How many thousands of God's people have been encouraged by these bold refrains of strong confidence in the protection of a caring God! Those who know these words—even people with little education or sophistication, full of age and weary of living—more distinctly know their God.

Consider again the lines:

Bless the LORD, O my soul:
and all that is within me, bless his holy name.
Bless the LORD, O my soul,
and forget not all his benefits (Ps. 103:1,2 KJV).

Or these:

Make a joyful noise unto the LORD,
all ye lands.
Serve the LORD with gladness:
come before his presence with singing (Ps. 100:1,2 KJV).

Or these:

I will lift up mine eyes unto the hills.
From whence cometh my help?
My help cometh from the LORD,
who made heaven and earth (Ps. 121:1,2 KJV, question
    mark added).

In fact, consider any of the familiar lines of the Psalter meditatively, and you will discover how appropriate they are in mirroring the variegated moods of the life of faith. We, who so often find our tongues stammering, our emotions choked, and our minds muddy, find our very necessary expressions of reality in these lines from the Psalms. Whether our mood is

19

blue or bright, whether we question God or confidently trust Him, whether we feel like singing or like weeping; we can do these in the Psalms.

AN AFFAIR OF THE HEART

This book comes out of a love affair that is deep and long-standing. I now wish to make it public. More than that, I wish to ask you to join with me in this love—in my love affair with the Book of Psalms!

This book is written for you who already love the Psalms, to encourage you in that love and to strengthen the bond. It is written for you if you only like the Psalms, to show you that your affection is too slight and to help you make a full embrace. Even if you are something of a stranger to the Psalms, this book is for you. It is high time for you to become more intimate with one of the richest of God's literary gifts. The psalmists encourage us to "taste and see that the Lord is good" (Ps. 34:8). His goodness will not be seen any better anywhere in the Old Testament than in the pages of His hymnic word.

What we wish to explore in this book is why the Psalms have such a fascination for those who have come to know them. We wish to learn *to feel with* the Psalms, *to share in* the songs of Israel's hymnbook, and *to participate in* these expressions of worship. Especially we wish to learn *to praise God* as only the Psalms can teach us to do.

CHAPTER 2

What Is a Psalm?

One way to begin a study of an Old Testament book is to examine the meaning of the *title* of that book. We may observe from our spelling of the word *Psalms* that this is not an English term. The initial "ps" tips us off.

THE TITLE *PSALMS* IS GREEK

The English word "psalms" is a transliteration of the Greek title of the book. That is, this is the Greek word simply spelled in English or Roman letters. The Greek word *psalmoi* was first translated into Latin as *Psalmi,* and then into English as "Psalms." The Greek word originally meant a *striking* or *twitching* of the fingers on a string. The related verb was used by classical writers for the "pulling of a bowstring." From that came the idea of "pulling or playing a stringed musical instrument."[1] When the word took on the extended meaning of a *song,* there was always the latent background of the stringed instrumental accompaniment tied to the singing. So the meaning of the Greek title of the book is "sacred songs sung to musical accompaniment."

We cannot escape from music in the Psalms! The emphasis upon music in the Psalter is seen in many Hebrew terms used in the superscriptions as well. The Hebrew words translated

[1]The Greek nouns are *psalmoi* (plural) and *psalmos* (singular). The related verb is *psallō.*

psalm and *song* are both terms of *music,* as is the common designation, "for the choir director," found in fifty-five Psalms.[2] Further, a number of Psalms specify instruments in their superscriptions (as Pss. 6,12), and perhaps also tunes or rhythmic patterns (as Pss. 45, 69, 80).

The Psalms are *music.* That is, they are the lyrics for the hymns of ancient Israel. The Church of Scotland, or Scots Kirk, has maintained this tradition by singing rhymed and metered versions of the Psalms in her hymnbooks. When we study the Psalms, it will help to remember that we are reading the words of Israel's hymns.

NEXT TO THEOLOGY IS MUSIC

I do not know how to emphasize sufficiently the importance of music in worship and in the life of the church. The fact that the longest book in the entire Bible is a book of *music* seems to have escaped the attention of many believers in the church today. How many pastors are there who give sufficient attention to the ministry of music in the worship of the congregation? How many leaders of music in the church truly have the desire to lead in worship? Truly to minister? Truly to honor God? How often do we realize in opening our hymnbooks that we are engaged in a sacred task, the adoration of God?

How scant is the attention given to church music in many theological seminaries! It is possible for a prospective pastor to complete both college and seminary training in many schools and never once be exposed to the role of music in church life. Given thought, this condition is an outrage against the history of the church, the heritage of the synagogue, and the prominent position of the Book of Psalms in the biblical canon.

---

[2]These Hebrew words are *mizmôr, šîr,* and *lamnaṣṣe(a)ḥ.* We shall see the importance of the superscriptions (the introductory words to the Psalms) a bit later.

Martin Luther once said that music is second only to theology in the service of God. According to Luther, "He who despises music . . . does not please me. Music is a gift of God, not a gift of men. . . . After theology I accord to music the highest place and the greatest honor."[3]

Of course, some of what slips by as music in the worship and adoration of the almighty God and Creator of the universe today seems a bit sleazy at best.

We must return to a biblical view of the role of music in worship. Music is not meant to be just a filler in the service to allow latecomers to find their places. It must be more than just an occasion for the congregation to stand before the "duration" of the sermon. Music provides opportunities for gifted soloists, trained ensembles, and the congregation as a whole to respond to God in a way that no other medium of expression allows.

The fact that the Psalms are *music without the notes,* however, means that for practical purposes the Psalms are *poems.* The tunes are lost to us, but the lyrics are what God has preserved. C. S. Lewis has written:

> What must be said . . . is that the Psalms are poems, and poems intended to be sung: not doctrinal treatises, nor even sermons. Those who talk of reading the Bible "as literature" sometimes mean, I think, reading it without attending to the main thing it is about; like reading Burke with no interest in politics, or reading the *Aeneid* with no interest in Rome. That seems to me to be nonsense. But there is a saner sense in which the Bible, since it is after all literature, cannot properly be read except as literature; and the different parts of it as the different sorts of literature they are. Most emphatically the Psalms must be read as poems; as lyrics, with all the licences and all the formalities, the hyperboles, the emotional rather than logical connections, which are proper to lyric poetry. They must be read as poems if they are to be understood; no less than French

[3]Cf. Ewald M. Plass, *What Luther Says: An Anthology,* 3 vols. (St. Louis: Concordia, 1959), vol. 2, p. 980.

must be read as French or English as English. Otherwise we shall miss what is in them and think we see what is not.[4]

The Greek title of the Book of Psalms, then, stresses the *poetic* and *musical* nature of the book.

A SCHOOL OF PRAYER

Having seen something of the significance of the Greek title, we may now turn to the Hebrew titles of the Psalter. One Hebrew title for the Psalms is suggested in the doxology to Book II: "The *prayers* of David the son of Jesse are ended" (Ps. 72:20 KJV, emphasis added). At one time in Israel's history there was a collection of Psalms ending with Psalm 72. This mini-collection was termed "The Prayers of David." This Hebrew word translated "prayers" is not the standard title of the book today, but it has a certain appropriateness.[5] Martin Luther found in the Psalms not only a great treasure of prophecies of Christ, but what he believed to be a school of prayer. He wrote:

> The Christian can learn to pray in the psalter, for here he can hear how the saints talk with God. The number of moods which are expressed here, joy and suffering, hope and care, make it possible for every Christian to find himself in it, and to pray with the psalms.[6]

Franz Delitzsch, a leading nineteenth century commen-

[4]C.S. Lewis, *Reflections on the Psalms* (New York: Harcourt, Brace & World, Inc. / A Harvest Book, 1958), pp. 2,3.

[5]This Hebrew word for "prayers" is *t^epillôt*.

[6]Cf. *Luther's Works,* ed. J.T. Pelikan and H.T. Lehmann, vol. 35, *Word and Sacrament,* vol. 1 (Philadelphia: Fortress, 1960), "Preface to the Psalter," pp. 254, 255ff.; cited by Otto Kaiser, *Introduction to the Old Testament: A Presentation of Its Results and Problems,* trans. John Sturdy (Minneapolis: Augsburg, 1975), p. 339. Five Psalms (Pss. 17,86,90,102,142) are termed "A Prayer" in their superscriptions.

tator on the Psalms, also spoke of a general appropriateness for "Prayers" as the Hebrew title. He wrote:

> The collective name *Tephilloth* [the Hebrew word] is suitable to all Psalms. The essence of prayer is a direct and undiverted looking towards God, and the absorption of the mind in the thought of Him. Of this nature of prayer all Psalms partake; even the didactic and laudatory, though containing no supplicatory address.[7]

Delitzsch then observed, as an example, that the Psalm of Hannah is introduced by the Hebrew verb translated "and she prayed" (1 Sam. 2:1). The relationship of praise and prayer is truly integral.

THE TITLE *PRAISES* IS HEBREW

However, it is *praise* rather than *prayer* that the Psalms are really about. The standard Hebrew title is the word that means "praises."[8] This designation is found only in the superscription to one Psalm (145), but it is the printed title for the entire book in the Hebrew Bible. Some writers, though, have questioned the appropriateness of this word for the collection. Delitzsch terms it only as "admissable."[9] Christoph Barth suggests it is "far from appropriate to every one of the hundred and fifty Psalms."[10]

The problem is one of finding a sufficiently comprehensive term to serve as the common denominator for all of the Psalms. The subject matter of these hymns is quite varied, and the moods are diverse. Some people who have had just a

[7]Franz Delitzsch, *Biblical Commentary on the Psalms,* trans. Francis Bolton, 3 vols. (Grand Rapids: Eerdmans, n.d.), vol. 1, p. 5.

[8]This Hebrew word for "praises" is *tᵉhillîm.*

[9]Delitzsch, *Psalms,* vol. 1, p. 5.

[10]Christoph F. Barth, *Introduction to the Psalms,* trans. R.A. Wilson (New York: Charles Scribners Sons, 1966), p. 1. He does later admit that this "traditional term comes nearer to the truth after all" (p. 2).

casual acquaintance with the Psalter seem to feel that these poems are all just about the same. But to those who have become endeared to the Psalms, there is a recognition of incredible variety and difference in the Psalms. Much like flakes of snow, the Psalms display great individuality. Each has been crafted lovingly by a master of design.

Yet there is one common element, as Claus Westermann has observed: The concept of *praise*. No matter how intense the hurt at the beginning of a Psalm of pain, ultimately the Psalm will lead to praise. So the Hebrew title is most appropriate. The Book of Psalms is the *Book of Praises*.

PRAISE: A NEED, NOT A FAD

As in the case of music so we may lament the vacuum of praise to God in many of our churches. The Book of Psalms exists as God's provision to teach us how to praise His name. In the book we learn spontaneity, specificity, intensity, and sincerity in praise. There are few things the modern church needs more.

I am aware that the recent history of the church has been beset with innumerable fads. One new idea about theology, methodology, lifestyle, and church life follows another. Each is presented with fanfare and excitement. Each flashes and splashes, then sparkles and sputters, and then is replaced by another new idea. We are weary with fads.

But the praise of God is not a passing fancy! It is one of the most elemental, fundamental, and necessary factors of the life of faith in this and any age. It is the goal and direction of all creation. The praise of God is the occupation of all His holy angels. The praise of God is the purpose of man. The praise of God is the end result of all God's wonders, all His being, and all His acts. If man will not praise God, the very stones will! (cf. Luke 19:40). He has redeemed us for the praise of His glory (cf. Eph. 1:6,12,14). This is no fad!

From the titles used for the Book of Psalms, we have seen that two principal factors emerge: The Greek title points to *music and poetry* and the Hebrew title points to *praise.* The Psalms are poems and are to be enjoyed as such. The *form* is music (in poetry), and the *substance* is praise. A Psalm is a poem that is sung as an expression of praise to God.

CHAPTER 3

How Is a Psalm?

I once saw a book entitled *How Is a Poem?* I first thought an error had been made in the title! Surely the title should read *What Is A Poem?* But the title was correct and good, for the concern of John Ciardi's book was to deal principally with *how* a poem is expressed rather than merely *what* a poem means.

THE FORMS OF OUR LIVES

You and I deal with forms all of our lives. Birth certificates, marriage licenses, death notices—these forms for hatching, matching, and dispatching mark our days. Grade reports, income tax returns, and plane tickets have their known characteristics.

In literature, music, and fine arts, there are forms as well. In music, for example, it does not take a Shostokovich to distinguish a march from a symphony, nor a Bix Beiderbeck to mark out Dixieland jazz from a concerto. Music has form; music *is* form. Even rock music has its cacophonous form, though some believe Euterpe, the muse of music, may never smile upon it!

On opening a letter, the reader can tell something of its form merely by the salutation: "Dear John. . ."; "Dear Sir, Am in receipt of yours of 9 October last . . ."; "My darling Coco-puff. . . ." In literature the form of a fairy tale is obvious from the beginning words, "Once upon a time. . . ." In poetry and verse the regular patterns of the elevated Petrarchan, or Italian, sonnet and the rhyme and rhythm of the lowly limerick are predictable. I will not take the space to quote a sonnet, but I cannot resist a limerick:

> A flea and a fly in a flue
> Were imprisoned so what could they do?
>   Said the flea, "Let us fly!"
>   Said the fly, "Let us flee!"
> So they flew through a flaw in the flue.

The distinctive rhyme and rhythmic patterns, the play on words (and the hint of "spice") all mark out the limerick as a distinct form.

Forms pervade our "electric literature" as well. Television was once described by Newton Minnow as a "vast wasteland." Yet it is not a wasteland without form. The early words of the Bible (Gen. 1:2) include the Hebrew phrase *tôhû-ve-vôhû,* meaning "formless and empty." Television is only *vôhû;* it may be empty at times, but it does have form. The soaps, sit-coms, and shoot-'em-ups all have their forms, as do the dramas, documentaries, and detective shows. There are patterns as well for the mini-productions that pay for it all, the commercials.

THE FORMS OF THE PSALMS

With forms all about us, it should come as no surprise that the Psalms have their forms as well. It is surprising, however, to learn how very recent is the rediscovery of these ancient forms. It was not until early in the present century that this particular area of biblical research began. The "father" of form criticism in the Old Testament was Hermann Gunkel. The importance of his contribution is great. Leopold Sabourin, a leading figure in Psalms research today, states that "Gunkel's method of classification, his insights into the history of the forms, their application to the Psalms, will remain the basis of all further studies."[1] More recently, Claus Westermann has modified and improved Gunkel's analyses in the book, *The Praise of God in the Psalms*.[2]

Some categories of the Psalms relate to content more than to pattern. These include the Royal Psalms, the Wisdom Psalms, and the Messianic Psalms. But some of the Psalms are best understood by applying the results of constructive form criticism. For example, one major group of Psalms expresses the sentiment that "God is good!" These are the *Praise Psalms*. Another group maintains, "But, life is tough!" These are the *Lament Psalms*. Let us look first at the Praise Psalms.

PSALMS OF PRAISE: GOD IS GOOD!

The Praise Psalms may be subgrouped under the titles *Descriptive Praise* or *Declarative Praise*. In Psalms of Descriptive Praise, the psalmist exults in the person of God, His sublime attributes, the glory of His name. These Psalms *describe* the God of praise. In the Psalms of Declarative Praise, the emphasis is on what God has done for His people. These *declare* the praise of God.

The patterns of these Praise Psalms are not complex. Basically they begin with a call to praise and then follow with a reason for that praise. Psalm 117, the briefest Psalm in the whole Psalter, shows this pattern most succinctly.[3]

[1]Leopold Sabourin, *The Psalms: Their Origin and Meaning,* enlarged ed. (Staten Island, N.Y.: Alba House, 1974) pp. 32–33. Gunkel's first study on the Psalms (*Ausgewahlte Psalmen*) was published in 1904. His *Introduction* (*Einleitung in die Psalmen*) was published in 1933. Barth, though, rightly cautions: "Even the best and most complete system [of form critical studies] will fail to include a considerable number of psalms, which it is either impossible to fit into any category, or which can be included only by a forced interpretation" (*Introduction,* p. 14).

[2]Trans. Keith R. Crim (Richmond, Va.: John Knox, 1965).

[3]All translations not otherwise labeled are my own.

A. *An Imperative to Praise Yahweh (v. 1)*
   Praise Yahweh all nations,
   Laud Him all tribes!

B. *The Motivation for the Praise of Yahweh (v. 2a, b)*
   For strong over us is His loyal love,
   And the steadfastness of Yahweh is forever!

C. *A Renewed Summons to Praise Yahweh (v. 2c)*
   Hallelujah (Praise Yah)!

In this powerful little Psalm, praise is commanded of all nations and all ethnic minorities. That is, the praise of God is a universal demand. This praise is based on Yahweh's extraordinary relationship with Israel, which ultimately brings blessing to all people (the outworking of the intent of the Abrahamic Covenant; see Gen. 12:1–3; Gal. 3:8). Without delaying here to expand on the theology of "one of the most potent and most seminal"[4] of the Psalms, we may observe this pattern: (1) an imperative to praise, (2) the motivation for praise, and (3) a renewed summons to praise God.

THE OLD ONE-HUNDRETH

Another illustration of this pattern is afforded by the *Jubilate* ("O be joyful!"), Psalm 100. Here there are four elements: (1) a summons to praise, (2) descriptive praise, (3) a renewed summons to praise, and (4) the motivation for praise. Basic to these Psalms are the commands to praise and the reasons for praise. Psalm 100 has expanded these elements somewhat.

As you read through this Psalm, consider your attitude about going to church. Is it merely to keep peace in the home? Is it just to set an example? Is it clothes to wear, contacts to

[4]Derek Kidner, *Psalms,* 2 vols. (Downers Grove, Ill.: Inter-Varsity, 1973, 1975), vol. 2, p. 412.

make, appearances to preserve? Is it a duty to perform, a pain to endure, a point to earn? *Or* is it unbounded joy at the opportunity to praise the living Yahweh in the community of the faithful? Only the last is the mood of this Psalm.

> Jesus is Lord!
> God is Good!
> We are the Redeemed!
> Praise His Name!

As you follow the *form* of Psalm 100, try not to miss the *mood*. Here is an outline of the Psalm:

PSALM 100

A Psalm for Public Acknowledgment

A. *A Summons to Praise Yahweh (vv. 1,2)*
   Shout joyfully to Yahweh all the earth!
   Serve Yahweh with delight;
   Come before Him with joyful, ringing sound.

The setting for this Psalm is in the community worship service, where the congregation is summoned to give a joyful, exultant praise of God. The verbs "come" (v. 2b) and "enter" (v. 4a, below) suggest the beginning of the praise service.

B. *Descriptive Praise of Yahweh (v. 3)*
   Know that Yahweh Himself is God;
   He has made us and His we are,
   His people, even the sheep of His pasture.

Here we have the main shout of praise, the *predication* (that which is preached). The statement of praise is, "Yahweh Himself is our God!" This is Israel's creed, reading out from the *Shema*^c (Deut. 6:4: "Hear, O Israel; Yahweh is our God, Yahweh alone!"). When Israel thought rightly, she never conceived of herself as a self-made people. She was Yahweh's distinct people, His creation, the sheep of His pasture.[5]

C. *A Renewed Summons to Praise Yahweh (v. 4)*
    Enter His gates with praise-offering,
    His courts with excited praise;
            Praise Him!
            Bless His Name!

[handwritten margin note: ascribe to God this characteristic, acknowledge, give thanks for them]

Often in praise Psalms the initial summons to praise will be renewed in the middle or even repeated at the end of the Psalm.

D. *The Motivation for Praise of Yahweh (v. 5)*
    For good is Yahweh;
    Everlasting is His loyal love,
    And for all generations is His faithfulness.

In these affirmations, which show the reasonableness of praise, the psalmist lauds Yahweh for three sublimities of His matchless character. *He is good!* Have you ever given thought to the possible consequences of a god who was not good, but evil? That is, what if there were one deity in the universe, and he were a malevolent god? Where then would we be? But in fact there is one God in the universe, and He is good! This is a prime reason to praise His name.

Not only is He good, but His *loyal love* and His *faithfulness* are for all generations. His loving relationship with the be-

---

[5]The second colon of this verse is translated in the KJV, "it is he that hath made us, and not we ourselves." Similarly the NASB ends this colon: "and not we ourselves." Nevertheless, "His we are" (see NASB margin) is preferable. This verse is one of fifteen in the Hebrew Old Testament where the word for "not" is confused with the word for "his" (both words sound alike). A *colon* is an accentual unit of Hebrew poetry. This verse has three *cola* (pl.), and is hence a line of *tricolon.*

liever lasts forever. He stakes His incomparable ethical character on maintaining this relationship for all time. Truly, praise is due His name!

Psalm 100 is a Psalm of *descriptive praise*. A few other Psalms in this category include Psalms 8, 29, 33, 36, 103–104, 105, 113, 135, 136, 145–150.

PSALMS OF LAMENT: LIFE IS TOUGH!

Many of the Psalms praise God for His goodness. But there are other moods in the Psalms as well. One dominant other voice says that *life is tough!* It is not easy to live the life of faith in a perverse and twisted society. When troubles come, our tendency is to set aside our praise of God and to sing harsh songs in minor keys, songs of stress, complaint, and lament. There are many such Psalms in the Bible. The *blues* may have been refined in the cotton fields of the Old South, but they *began* among God's people Israel in the pastures of ancient Palestine.

Perhaps the most important observation you should make in reading these Psalms of Lament is that *finally they too lead to praise.*

The *Psalms of Lament* are subdivided by the *number* in the personal pronouns involved. Those Psalms that use the *plural* pronoun, such as Psalms 44, 60, 74, 79, 80, 83, 85, 90, 123, and 137 (and perhaps a few others) are termed *Laments of the People,* or *Laments of the Community.* Those Psalms such as 3, 5, 6, 7, 13 (and many others, see note 11, page 39) that use the *singular* pronoun are termed *Laments of the Individual.*

Since the Laments comprise the larger number of Psalms in the collection, when viewed in terms of form criticism, an understanding of the pattern will be of inestimable value as an interpretive aid. The form is more complex than that of the Psalms of Descriptive Praise. There are six elements in more or less regular sequence and occurrence. These are: (1) the introductory appeal, (2) the lament, (3) the confession of trust, (4) the petition, (5) the motifs that may justify divine intervention, and (6) the vow of praise or the shout of praise. In some Psalms of this category there is a seventh element: (7) the prophetic utterance.

The psalmists were never bound or locked into the forms, or patterns, but they used them to their best advantage. A fine example is afforded by Psalm 6, one of the seven "Penitential Psalms" (others are Pss. 32,38,51,102,130,143). Here is this Psalm in schematic display. (You may wish to have your Bible open as you read these notes.)

PSALM 6
For the choir director:
with stringed instruments, upon an eight stringed lyre
A Psalm of David

A. *Introductory Appeal*
In verse 1 this element is given in these words:

O Yahweh, do not rebuke me in Your anger,
Nor in Your wrath chastise me.

B. *The Lament*
The lament may be expressed in terms of three pronouns:

I am hurting;
You are not helping;
They are winning.

1. In Psalm 6 *the "I" element* is prominent in the words:

I am pining away . . .
My bones are dismayed . . .
My soul is greatly dismayed (vv. 2,3).

This "I" section is further emphasized in verses 6,7:

> I am weary with my sobbing;
> Every night I make my bed swim,
> I dissolve my couch with my tears.
> My eye has wasted away with grief;
> It has become old because of all my adversaries.

These bold hyperboles are most powerful in evoking the feeling of distress on the part of the psalmist.

2. *The "You" element* in this Psalm is suggested in the first verse, that God's anger *does* rebuke the psalmist and that His wrath *does* presently chasten him. The accusational "You" element is made startlingly abrupt in verse 3b:

> But You, O Yahweh—how long?

That is, do You not care? Will You not act? Soon? Ever? The words "how long?" express the plaintive charge in many of these Psalms of individual lament.[6]

3. *The "they" element* is only implied in the early verses, but the enemy is noted expressly in verse 7b, "all my adversaries." Other Psalms magnify the enemy aspect. Psalm 12, for example, has a moving emphasis on the enemy and his deceitful tongue (see Ps. 12:2–4).

C. *The Confession of Trust*
The psalmist implies his residual trust in Yahweh with the words of verse 4b:

> . . . on the basis of your loyal love.

[6]Quite another use of "how long?" is found in the lament of the martyrs of Revelation 6:10, "How long, O Lord, holy and true, wilt Thou refrain from judging and avenging our blood on those who dwell on the earth?" (NASB).

Furthermore, he employs the divine name *Yahweh* four times in verses 1–3. By using God's *name,* David is asserting his ultimate confidence, even in distress. Psalm 5, which is similar in structure, has a forceful statement of trust: "My King and my God!" (v. 2).

D. *The Petition*

This is usually given in strong imperatives, and in some Psalms there is a three-fold development, as follows:

Listen! In Psalm 5:2, "Heed the sound of my cry!"

Save! In Psalm 5:8, "Lead me in Your righteousness!"

Punish! In Psalm 5:10, "Hold them guilty!"

In Psalm 6 the verbs of petition are found in verse 4:

Listen! "Return!"

Save! "Rescue my life!"

Save! "Save me!"

(A statement of vengeance is lacking in this Psalm, so the "save" shout is given with two verbs.)

E. *The Motivational Motifs*

The pathos of the petition is often heightened by motifs designed to make the petition reasonable and to compel Yahweh to vindicate His name. In verse 5 David suggests that if Yahweh does not come to his aid, the psalmist's life will be in danger and Yahweh may lose his praise on this earth:

For there is no mention of You in death;
In Sheol who gives You praise?

These lines should not be read as a theology of death, but as a theology of praise. It is not that one is unconscious in death but in death the believer is lost to the community in its praise of God. Dahood, following Brevard S. Childs, summarizes this well: "The psalmist suffers not because of the inability to remember Yahweh in Sheol, but from being unable to share in the praise of Yahweh which characterizes Israel's worship."[7]

F. *The Vow of Praise/The Shout of Praise*
In this Psalm, as in a number of others (e.g., Pss. 13,22,28,31, and 56), there is a remarkable change of mood at the end of the poem. A number of unsatisfactory cultic and psychological explanations have been suggested for these dramatic shifts from pain to praise.[8] That which seems to have happened, however, is that God has "burst" into the Psalm through a prophetic oracle or a priestly response. Westermann suggests that "in some instances it is to be assumed that an oracle of salvation was given in the *midst* of the Psalm and that the Psalm also includes the words that follow the giving of the oracle."[9] Hence, the psalmist states his praise with boldness, condemning his enemy and magnifying his great God:

> Depart from me, all you who practice iniquity,
> For Yahweh has heard the sound of my weeping.
> Yahweh has heard my supplication;
> Yahweh received my prayer (vv. 8,9).[10]

The psalmist's suffering at the beginning of the Psalm was terribly intense; his joy at the conclusion is no less so. *How remarkable this is!* God *has* stooped to the needs of a hurting believer.

In Psalm 6, to repeat, *praise occurs* because God already has answered. In Psalm 142, by contrast, God has not yet

[7]Mitchell Dahood, *The Anchor Bible: Psalms I* (Garden City, N.Y.: Doubleday, 1965), p. 38.

[8]Some of these views on what might be termed "the spiritual yo-yo syndrome" in the Psalms are summarized by Kaiser, *Introduction,* p. 335.

[9]Westermann, *Praise of God,* p. 65; a similar statement is given by Barth, *Introduction,* p. 16.

[10]The verb "received" is likely a Hebrew preterite (prefixed tense) without the *waw* and is to be translated as a past narrative, not as a future ("will receive" KJV) or present ("receives" NASB). See Dahood, *Psalms I,* p. 39.

responded, so the last section of that Psalm will be seen to contain a *vow to praise* God when the psalmist will have been delivered (v. 7).

G. *The Prophetic Utterance*
Psalm 6 adds to the praise of God an utterance of confidence based on God's response in which the psalmist describes the terrible end of his enemies:

> All my enemies shall be ashamed and greatly dismayed;
> They shall turn back, they shall suddenly be ashamed (v. 10).

Here the psalmist uses terminology for his enemy that he formerly used to describe his own plight (see v. 2b, "dismayed"). In other Psalms of this class there is a final judgment against the enemy. For example, Psalm 141:10 reads:

> Let the wicked fall into their own nets,
> While I pass by safely.

An understanding of this basic pattern will be a most significant aid in reading and understanding the large number of laments of the individual in the Psalter.[11]

READ! SING! PRAISE!

For years Billy Graham has urged his hearers to take a month aside for special Bible reading and devotions. In this month he suggests that you read one chapter a day in the Book of Proverbs and five chapters a day in the Book of

[11]Sabourin (*The Psalms,* p. 218) generously list the following: Pss. 5–7,13,17,25,26,28,31,35,38,39,42,43,51,54,55,57,59,61,64,69,70,71,86, 88,102,109,120,130,140,143 and possibly Pss. 22,36, and 63.

Psalms, enabling you to complete both books in the month. You will have to rise early on the twenty-fourth, however, as that will be the day for Psalm 119.

The reading of the Proverbs will aid you in your relationships with other people. The chapters in the Psalms will guide you in your relationship with God. The balance in the two books could not be better.

You may have heard Mr. Graham make this suggestion many times in the past. Have you ever done it? May I add my words of encouragement? You may really like it!

From here on as you read this book, start to read the Psalms themselves. Begin with Psalm 1. You have enough information before you to enjoy the Psalms in a new way. Read them slowly. Read them aloud. Read them with sensitivity. Listen to them sing! Follow them as they display the conventions of an ancient age. Learn from the psalmists the praise of the living Yahweh!

CHAPTER 4

Poetry—
The Language of the Psalms

There is no easy way of backing into the subject matter of this chapter. We now need to face an issue squarely: *The Psalms are written in poetry,* and poetry seems to have few friends today. For many, poetry smacks of elitism, snobbery, or irrelevance. Football mania and the "electric carrot," as Bruce Lockerbie describes television, conspire against time for, or interest in, the gentle art of reading poetry.

Calling poetry a gentle art is, however, somewhat deceptive. For to learn to read poetry is not a passive task. Reading poetry is an "active sport." We sometimes seem too schooled in passive media as mere observers to have an interest in the active and demanding task of *participation* that a poem entails.

The Psalms were written by poets. The Psalms *are* poetry. C. S. Lewis insisted that the Psalms *must* be read as poems if they are to be understood. This means that it may well be appropriate to generalize a bit on poetry itself, for there are many misapprehensions concerning the nature of poetry that will halt our progress if they are not promptly checked. You need to exercise your will from this day on to *like* poetry.

POETRY AND VERSE

Were a poll to be taken concerning the average reader's view of poetry, I suspect that the result would be a consensus that poetry is a literature that has rhyme and rhythm.

Many poems certainly have fixed rhyme and regular rhythm. But Hebrew poetry lacks these two features that seem so common to English poetry. The sophisticated reader, however, is well aware that what many call poetry is only verse. Simply putting words into nice accentual units and arranging them with end-line rhymes is not to write poetry. The outstanding professor emeritus of literature at the University of Southern California, Dr. Frank Baxter, has said that the following verse has some of the most beautiful words in the English language:

Thirty days hath September
April, June and November;
All the rest have thirty-one,
Excepting February alone,
And that has twenty-eight days clear
And twenty-nine in each leap year.

This verse has a great beauty of sound. It has clear rhyme and rhythm. But these pretty words do not make a *poem*. They are merely pretty verse. Verse has rhyme and rhythm; poetry has *more*. Much of the sentiment of greeting cards is verse; little of it is poetry. Those flirtatious notes in the school annual are likely doggerel, not poetry either.

MESSAGE AND BEAUTY

If poetry is more than verse, what is it? Before answering this, however, we should address two further misconceptions concerning poetry: the issues of message and beauty. It is believed by many that a poem must have a clear message. It is also assumed that the appropriate response on the hearing of a poem is to cluck-cluck a bit, and then to twitter, "That is so beautiful!" As a matter of fact, a poem can be great literature and have neither a message nor a "pretty" quality.

Read this song from Shakespeare to see these elements.

WINTER

When icicles hang by the way,
  And Dick the shepherd blows his nail,
And Tom bears logs into the hall,
  And milk comes frozen home in pail,
When blood is nipped and ways be foul,
Then nightly sings the staring owl,
               "To-whit, to-who!"
A merry note,
While greasy Joan doth keel the pot.

When all aloud the wind doth blow,
  And coughing drowns the parson's saw,
And birds sit brooding in the snow,
  And Marian's nose looks red and raw,
When roasted crabs hiss in the bowl,
Then nightly sings the staring owl,
               "To-whit, to-who!"
A merry note,
While greasy Joan doth keel the pot.

Laurence Perrine quotes this poem in his *Sound and Sense: An Introduction to Poetry.*[1] He observes that this poem obviously contains no moral, nor is the poem especially pretty or beautiful in the usual sense of these words. There is little that is attractive in coughing, greasy Joan, red hands, foul roads, and a runny nose!

THE LANGUAGE OF EXPERIENCE

Nevertheless, "Winter" is a splendid poem. It does what a poem is intended to do: It communicates *experience.* Literature is a language of experience, and poetry is the most concentrated form of literature. Poetry is therefore the most powerful literary means of expressing experience. By reading

[1]Laurence Perrine, *Sound and Sense: An Introduction to Poetry,* 3rd ed. (New York: Harcourt, Brace & World, 1961), see pp. 3–11.

this poem, one who lives far away from a sixteenth-century English country house is able to experience winter in such a time and location.

Poetry is a special use of language. Perrine remarks that "poetry might be defined as a kind of language that says more and says it *more intensely* than does ordinary language."[2] Poetry is not designed basically to communicate information. One might wind up with a rather grotesque contraption were he to use a poem to build a barn. I would not wish to drive a car that was repaired by a mechanic on the basis of a poem. One might drown if he used a poem to learn how to swim. A good poem might, however, give me an experience of being in a barn, or driving, or swimming that could be intense and satisfying. Poetry is the language of experience. It is powerful in its communicative ability.

Consider this poem by Alfred Tennyson:

THE EAGLE

He clasps the crag with crooked hands;
Close to the sun in lonely lands,
Ringed with the azure world, he stands.

The wrinkled sea beneath him crawls;
He watches from his mountain walls,
And like a thunderbolt he falls.

There are many ways to learn about eagles. We might look in a book on zoology or read an article in a dictionary. We might visit a zoo or a desert crag. But in this poem by Lord Tennyson, we may have an experience of "eagleness" that is valid and profound. The first stanza presents the lonely vigil of the eagle in the world of blue, sun, and desert mountains. The second stanza shows his perspective: He is so high that the sea seems to be wrinkled and crawling. Then the sudden,

[2]Ibid., p. 4.

majestic, and deadly flight of the eagle shatters our reverie in an explosion of motion.

Yet there is no real message in the poem "The Eagle." A poem *may* have a message (and the poems of the Bible certainly do). But it is a mistake to look first and foremost for the message, and *miss the experience*. I do not know if books on biblical hermeneutics (the art and science of Bible interpretation) emphasize this clearly enough. Were it only the *message* that God intended us to receive from a given passage, He might have used language that was far clearer. The fact that He has sanctioned the use of poetry as a means of revelation suggests that the *experience* is also quite important.

HANGING AROUND WORDS

John Ciardi cites an anecdote by W. H. Auden on the relative importance of the message of a poem. Auden was asked a question on how he might advise a young person who wished to become a poet. Auden's reply was that he would ask the young person why he wanted to write poetry. Ciardi reports:

> If the answer was "because I have something important to say," Auden would conclude that there was no hope for that young man as a poet. If on the other hand the answer was something like, "because I like to hang around words and overhear them talking to one another," then that young man was at least interested in a fundamental part of the poetic process and there was hope for him.[3]

In view of the special nature of Hebrew poetry, I find the words to Auden by the second would-be poet most appropriate. Hebrew poetry is based on listening to words talking to

[3]John Ciardi, *How Does a Poem Mean?* Part Three of *An Introduction to Literature* by Herbert Barrows, Hubert Heffner, John Ciardi, and Wallace Douglas (Boston: Houghton Mifflin, 1959), p. 361.

each other. We need to learn to "hang around" these words and hear what it is they say to each other.

Poetry is to be *felt*. So intensely does he feel certain poems that Frank Baxter says that there are some poems he simply cannot think of while shaving in the morning or he will surely nick himself. Our reaction to the reading of the Psalms ought to be such that we *feel* with them so deeply that we cannot think of these words without some response.

A THEOLOGY OF BEAUTY

The common response of a casual reader of poetry might be "Isn't that beautiful!" Some who read a poem and make that exclamation may really mean, "Isn't that pretty!" That is, they may be captivated with the superficial in the absence of the sublime. The Christian reader of poetry needs to have a theology of beauty that is consequent with his or her Christian faith, and which is in accord with the Scriptures. Frank E. Gaebelein, headmaster emeritus of the Stony Brook School in New York, deals with the importance of a right understanding of beauty in art. He states:

> To identify beauty with what is immediately pleasing or captivating is to have a superficial view of beauty. The difference between a Rembrandt portrayal of Christ and one by Sallman is the difference between depth and superficiality.[4]

He then observes that there is more to beauty than mere orderliness and harmony. "The concept of beauty in art must be large enough to include the aesthetic astringencies," he says.[5] Art may be characterized by serenity, but it may also be rugged and thorny.

[4]Frank E. Gaebelein, "What Is Truth in Art?" *Christianity Today* (August 27, 1976), p. 13.
[5]Ibid.

Gaebelein proposes four marks of truth in art that may aid the Christian in confronting art. These are: (1) durability, (2) unity, (3) integrity, and (4) inevitability. These are guides for the appreciation of any form of art, and they have a direct application to the appreciation of poetry.

A great poem will not be tissue art, to be used and then discarded; a great poem we may expect will last. A great poem will not be a patchwork quilt with no discernible unity; a poem of artistic level will display unity. A poem of theological merit will certainly demonstrate integrity. It may be *wrong* to be pretty, if in prettiness the truth is distorted. Finally, a great poem will have about it a sense of inevitability. At the end of the experience of reading the poem, the reader responds, "This is right; this is the way it has to be."[6]

POETRY AND SCRIPTURE

If the values in poetry in general are true values, then the poetry of the Scriptures is most valuable indeed. A good poet may write a great poem that may in fact communicate an experience that is base, misunderstood, twisted, or corrupt. In doing so, this poet may violate the criterion of integrity as determined by the Scriptures. The poets of the Bible have written poetry that communicates truth and beauty of the highest order because of the direction and inspiration of the Spirit of God.

In our emphasis that poetry communicates experience, we should not imply that the poetry of the Bible does not also have a great message. Assuredly it does! God used the poets of Israel to communicate great content through the vehicle of significant art. Francis A. Schaeffer explains it this way:

[6]These four characteristics are developed by Gaebelein on pages 11–12 of his article. Another helpful list of criteria for judging art was suggested by Francis A. Schaeffer in his book, *Art and the Bible* (London: Hodder and Stoughton, 1973). These are the four standards: "(1) technical excellence, (2) validity, (3) intellectual content, the world view which comes through, and (4) the integration of content and vehicle" (p. 39).

Some years ago a theologian at Princeton commented that he did not mind saying the creeds, provided he could sing them. What he meant was that so long as he could make them a work of art he didn't feel he had to worry about the content. But this is poor theology and poor aesthetics. A lyric can contain considerable theological content. An epic can be as emphatically (and accurately) historic as a straight piece of prose. Just because something takes the form of a work of art does not mean it cannot be factual.[7]

With this background, we are now more prepared to think of the more particular nature of the poetry of the Old Testament.

REDISCOVERING HEBREW POETRY

It was surprisingly late in the history of the church that the nature of Hebrew poetry was finally rediscovered. This was done by an English bishop who was professor of poetry at Oxford University. In 1753 Bishop Robert Lowth discovered the genius of Hebrew poetry, which he called *parallelism*. This date, 1753, is, of course, long after the publication of the King James Version (KJV) of 1611. This means that despite the lovely cadance, the beautiful expression of language, and the splendid work of translation that we find in the KJV, that translation was done by scholars who lived before the discovery of the basic elements of Hebrew poetry.[8]

This unfortunate lack of knowledge on the part of the translators of the King James Bible shows itself most prominently in the typesetting. The typesetters have put every verse into a sentence paragraph, with the words running

[7]Schaeffer, *Art and the Bible*, p. 46. For these reasons we ought to drop that cliché, "There is more truth in that than poetry."

[8]Christoph Barth says, "Anyone who knows the psalms only from Luther's Bible, the Authorized Version or the Prayer Book, or any such older translation, does not realize he is reading poetry—that the psalms are in fact *poems* in the strict sense." *Introduction*, p. 9.

from margin to margin. By looking at a page, one cannot readily tell if it is poetry or prose. One has to be told that parts of the Bible are in poetry. For the typesetting alone, the newer translations of the Bible such as the New American Standard Bible (NASB) and the New International Version (NIV) are greatly helpful. In part to meet the need of the readers of the KJV for a visual impression of poetry, a new edition is underway, the New King James Bible (NKJB, Thomas Nelson Publishers). In this printing the poetry will be shown in a satisfactory format.

That the Book of Psalms is poetry is clear. But much of the rest of the Old Testament is also poetry. In addition to books such as Proverbs, Ecclesiastes, the Song of Solomon, and Job, large sections of the prophetic books are poetry as well. I remember hearing a sermon one time in which a well-meaning preacher was attacking the relatively new Revised Standard Version (RSV) of the Old Testament because of certain deficiencies he saw in it. One of his less memorable attacks, however, was the charge: "And not only that, they have turned the Book of Isaiah into poetry!" Well, it was Isaiah who wrote the poetry. The RSV translators simply arranged the words on the page so that the book could be read as poetry. Perhaps one fourth of the Old Testament is poetry. We *must* learn to read poetry well if we are to read the Bible well!

THE POETRY OF CANAAN

Lowth's work has been advanced dramatically in the last half century. One of the major aids for scholars in their growing understanding of the nature of Hebrew poetry has been the research in the poetic texts from Ugarit. Ugaritic is the name of the language of a most important text discovery made in northern Syria in 1928. A Syrian peasant plowing with a wooden plow, iron bit, and a stubborn donkey found himself stuck by a large rock. He must have said some terrible things in Arabic as he struggled to move the stone. But he found a hole which led to the discovery of an ancient city. Trained archaeologists rushed to the site, and ancient Ugarit was discovered at modern Ras Shamra in northern Syria.

The people of Ugarit were Canaanites, although they were far enough north of Canaan that their culture was somewhat mixed and cosmopolitan. Among the large holdings of dockets, economic texts, and the like were three major poetic texts. These epics are known as "The Legend of Keret," "Baal and Anat," and "The Epic of Aqhat." The language of Ugarit is quite closely related to biblical Hebrew, although its alphabet is written in cuneiform (wedge-shaped) signs.

Of special significance was the discovery that the poetry of Ugarit is the same kind of poetry that we have in the Bible. These texts date back to 1500 B.C., with the latest texts from 1200 B.C. when the city was destroyed by an earthquake. The study of the poetry of Ugarit has been of incomparable value in explaining the poetry of the Old Testament.

For example, it is found that many of the synonyms used in parallelism in the Bible are the precise terms used in the ancient Ugaritic poetry. One conclusion based on these old poetic traditions is quite significant. It is no longer possible for a critic of the Bible to say that the poetry of the Old Testament could not have been written by David or anyone else so early in Israel's history because the poetic art must have been too crude at that rustic an age. The poetry from Ugarit has demonstrated, among other things, that the poetic traditions in Israel are part of a larger and more ancient cultural mold. David is still the "sweet singer of Israel" we believe him to be. But his kind of singing is far older than we might have imagined.

THE STEREO IN YOUR BIBLE

Now let us look at the precise nature of biblical poetry. Bishop Lowth was the first to enunciate the basic element of Hebrew poetry. It is not rhyme nor fixed meter, but *paral-*

lelism. Parallelism is one statement followed by another, done with art, style, and image. That is, by saying the same thing in slightly different words, the total impression is enhanced beyond saying either line alone.

Parallelism in Hebrew poetry may be compared to a stereophonic music system. In fact, a better word for our day than parallelism may be *stereometrics*.[9] As one listens to a stereo recording he receives from the two speakers together a "living" sensation of the sound. So the ancient poets by using two channels, as it were, communicate in brilliantly living sound.

The devices of parallelism that the poets of the Bible used are varied. We may survey them briefly. In each case, imagine the first line to be coming from one stereo speaker and the second from the other speaker. Ask, as you read, what impression the lines make *together* beyond what either says alone.

Synonymous parallelism

In this type of parallelism, the first line is echoed in the second, with a slight change of terms. The parallels are not to be thought of as mathematical equals; the precision of the poet is of a different sort. Examples (all from the Psalms) include the following:

Why are the nations in an uproar,
And the peoples devising a vain thing? (2:1).

O Yahweh, how my adversaries have increased!
Many are rising up against me (3:1).

[9]I first discovered this happy word in Gerhard von Rad's *Wisdom in Israel*, trans. James D. Martin (Nashville: Abingdon, 1972), p. 27, note 5 (quoting B. Landsberger). Von Rad says of this phenomenon that "it offers the poet virtually inexhaustible possibilities of inflection of poetic thought" (p. 27). When Landsberger used the word his model was visual stereometry; I have opted for stereophonics for my model.

Antithetical parallelism

In an antithetical parallel the words of the first line are affirmed in the second, not by repetition of a similar thought, but by the denial of the opposite. Here are some examples:

> For Yahweh knows the way of the righteous,
> But the way of the wicked will perish (1:6).

> How blessed is the man who has made
>   Yahweh his trust,
> And has not turned to the proud, nor to those
>   who lapse into falsehood (40:4).

We may observe in these examples the extra dimension as the words play against each other. The contrasts in the first verse imply that Yahweh does *not* know the way of the wicked and that the way of the righteous will endure. In the second verse the contrasts imply a curse on the one who does not make Yahweh his trust, whereas the faithfulness of God is stressed in the contrast with the proud and the false.

Here is a more complicated example, where the first verse is in synonymous parallelism as is the second, but the two verses together are antithetical:

> For I will not trust in my bow,
> Nor will my sword save me.

> But You have saved us from our adversaries,
> And You have put to shame those who hate us (44:6,7).

Climactic parallelism

This is a refinement and development of synonymous parallelism in which the second line takes some words from the first, but then completes the idea left unfulfilled in the first line. For example:

Ascribe to Yahweh, O sons of the mighty,
Ascribe to Yahweh glory and strength (96:7).

Synthetic parallelism

Here is another refinement of synonymous parallelism. In this type the second line develops the thought of the first line a bit further, adding details or dimension, but not quoting words from it as in climactic parallelism. Here are examples:

For Yahweh is a great God,
And a great King above all gods (95:3).

Come let us worship and bow down;
Let us kneel before Yahweh our Maker (95:6).

Emblematic parallelism

In this type of parallelism, the first line may have a figure of speech that is explained in the second line. Poetry of all nations contains vivid figures of speech and word pictures. Hebrew poetry too delights in such. Here is an example:

As the deer pants for the water brooks,
So my soul pants for You, O God (42:1).

This great image shows at once the believer's desire to be in the courts of worship as well as his frustration in his wary walk, as he is pursued by his enemies. In some cases the second line has the figure of speech:

Your tongue devises destruction,
Like a sharp razor, O worker of deceit (52:2).

Formal relationship

When a verse has two parts, but no clearly discernible parallelism is evident, scholars speak of a "formal" relationship. In another context these verses might be prose; in a poem they help to add variety and an unexpectedness to the lines of frequent parallelism. Here are some examples:

> Forever, O Yahweh,
> Your word is settled in heaven (119:89).

> O God of my praise,
> Do not be silent! (109:1).

THE UNIVERSAL POETRY

These are the more obvious features of Hebrew poetry. Since parallelism, or stereometrics, is the essential genius of Hebrew poetry, it is especially providential that this is *the very thing* that does not suffer in translation. Were Hebrew poetry based on rhyme and regular metrical patterns, translation into the major languages of the world would be stilted and imprecise because of the difficulties of rendering such poetry into the receiving or target language idiom.

My wife and I enjoy attending the opera. Before going to an operatic performance we try to study the libretto, particularly if the opera is to be sung in Italian or another foreign language. The libretti are published with the original words in one column and the English translation in another. It is often amusing to see how much different the English poetic version is from the original, simply because the translator had to search for rhyme and rhythm patterns that would fit.

But the essential poetic element in the Old Testament can be rendered into any target language without any compromise of integrity. Kidner says of the poetry of the Old Testament that "it is well fitted by God's providence to invite 'all the earth' to 'sing the glory of his name.' "[10] This is truly providential, and it is wonderful.[11]

[10]Kidner, *Psalms I*, p. 4.
[11]The poetry of the Qur'an is another matter. Strict Muslims oppose any translation of the holy book of Islam, so important are rhyme and rhythm in this literature in the original Arabic.

LET THE BIBLE LIVE!

Despite the rediscovery of Hebrew poetry, the real beauty of this literature is not always appreciated. We *do* live in an age that is not conducive to poetry! Perhaps because of a lack of general sensitivity, or of training, or of time, or perhaps because an exaggerated and distorted sense of "practicality" has had its sway, not many have learned to enjoy the poetry of the Bible. Unfortunately, some of the translations we use are partially responsible.

With a desire to make the Bible more understandable to some people, our popular paraphrases of the Bible often reduce the exciting life of the poetry to cold and simple prose. If one desires to read prose, the Bible is filled with prose texts. But the poetry of the Bible must be allowed to *sing,* for it is one of God's gifts to us.

THE REAL THING

We have some dear friends who revolted quite suddenly and completely against our modern plastic-wrapped food supply. No more additives! No more sugar! No more monosodium glutamate! And, especially, no more bleached and refined flour!

After a week or so of their new diet, the three young boys in the family were about to stage a revolt of their own because of the unfamiliar heavier and darker breads and such. Things came to a head one day when their mother bought some eggs from us at our little farmlet. When she opened this carton of fresh, brown-shelled eggs, she saw her young boys gasp in frustration. "Oh, no!" one boy said to his brothers. "Now we even have to eat whole wheat eggs!"

Sometimes we find ourselves so used to "plastic" substitutes, we do not know how to relate to "the real thing." Since God was pleased to communicate so much of His Word through gifted poets, it follows that we must be willing to learn to read with profit and understanding the poetic literature if we are to benefit from these texts. Further, since poetry is the language of experience, what we have to gain by a careful and sensitive reading of the poems of the Psalter is *an indelible and authentic experience with God.*

If we wish to have an experience with God that is unquestionably valid, true, and authentic—God has prepared it for us in the experiential language of the Psalms.

CHAPTER 5

Praise—
The Center of the Psalms

The Book of Psalms centers in the praise of God. We have seen that the Greek title of the book points to the poetry and music of the Psalms. The Hebrew title of the book is the word *tᵉhillîm,* "Praises."

I have found it quite remarkable that the one who has done so much to recover the praise-centeredness of the Psalms did so while *in the depths.* Claus Westermann was interned in a German prison camp during the Second World War. He had with him only Luther's translation of the New Testament and the Book of Psalms. In his experience in a concentration camp, Westermann learned how to praise God![1] One who has so learned praise will not soon balk at a lament in the Psalter.

---

[1]This is noted on the dust jacket of his book *The Praise of God in the Psalms.* His experiences may also be referred to in the "Preface" (pp. 9–11), where he speaks of a congregation during the war years learning to praise God. He writes, "In such praise out of the depths, their need, the sorrow through which they had to struggle all alone, was no longer merely their own concern. It was not *merely* a test and confirmation of their piety, a happening that took place between God and their soul, but it was an occurrence in the congregation" (p. 9). He then writes: "Whenever one in his enforced separation praised God in song, or speech, or silence, he was conscious of himself not as an individual, but as a member of the congregation. When in hunger and cold, between interrogations, or as one sentenced to death, he was privileged to praise God, he knew that in all his ways he was borne up by the church's praise of God. By this it became an element of what was going on between God and the world. . . . This praise out of the depths has become an argument that speaks louder than the arguments that we have been accustomed to bring forth for 'Christendom' " (p. 10).

TOWARDS A DEFINITION OF PRAISE

Webster's New World Dictionary of the American Language gives three meanings for the verb "to praise." These are as follows: (1) originally "to set a price on," "to appraise"; (2) the next meaning grew from this: "to commend the worth of," "to express approval or admiration of"; and (3) finally there came the meaning: "to laud the glory of (God, etc.), as in song," "to glorify," "to extol." That is, *praise concerns speaking well of, to extol the virtues of, to magnify.*

The Psalms command, enjoin, encourage, and exemplify the praise of God. They serve as the textbook on praise. What we find in the Psalms concerning praise intensifies the English word "praise," for the Psalms suggest that praise is *a matter of life and breath.* That is, praise must come from a genuine and vital relationship with God, and praise to God must be vocal and in a public forum. Praise is not silent nor is praise possible in solitude. Praise cannot be artificial or by rote either. A. H. Leitch states:

> The glory and majesty of God and all His works are to fill men's hearts and find expression in their word and witness. This becomes so over-powering to a man's mind and heart that he must break out in some utterance.[2]

WHY BE SILENT?

To say that praise must be genuine should cause no offense. But I suspect that there may be some question as to why I would stress that praise must be vocal and public. We are accustomed to hearing instructions respecting prayer such as, "Now all silently praise God" or "When you have your quiet time, do not forget to praise God." Not only have we learned from such expressions, many of us have used similar

[2]A.H. Leitch, "Praise," in Merrill F. Tenney, ed., *The Zondervan Pictorial Bible Encyclopedia,* vol. 4, p. 834.

terminology ourselves. Nevertheless, strictly speaking, the Old Testament concept of praise does not fit into our idioms of silent prayer and quiet times.

If praise involves sound, why then do our choirs often begin a worship service with the introit: "The Lord is in His holy temple./Let all the earth be silent before Him"? Perhaps this is done because some of our Protestant churches are notoriously noisy at the beginning of a service. They are noisy usually with chatter, not with the praise of God. What's a choir director to do? When the organ begins to play, the buzzing of the congregation just gets louder to compensate for it. The choir director has to call for order. Instead of banging a judicial gavel, he hushes the congregation by a choral admonition.

Nevertheless, the context of the words sung by the choir (see Hab. 2:20) is that of judgment, not worship. It is a call of a wrathful Deity for sinners who reject Him to "hush!" God is about to exercise vengeance! The Hebrew word translated "be silent" is an example of onomatopoeia, a word imitating a sound, such as our word "buzz." This Hebrew word is *haś*. It is the same word exactly as our "hush!"

The same Hebrew term is used in an identical type of judgmental context in Zechariah 2:13:

> Be silent [*haś*] all flesh, before Yahweh;
> For He is aroused from His holy habitation.

Yet immediately before these words calling for silence on the part of those to be judged, Israel is told:

> Sing for joy and be glad, O daughter Zion;
> For behold I am coming and I will dwell in your midst—
> declares Yahweh (v. 10).

Again, Zephaniah 1:7 calls upon a world about to be judged to "hush!"

Be silent [haś] before the Lord Yahweh!
For the day of Yahweh is near;
For Yahweh has prepared a sacrifice,
He has consecrated His guests.

The verses that follow this text are sprinkled with words for punishment, devastation, violence, and judgment by God. Those who are told to "hush" will actually speak. But their vocabulary will be words of wailing, moaning, and despair.

So it stands true. Praise is vocal. Man is called to be silent when God is about to wreak His vengeance on an unrepentant world. Church congregations should be silent at the beginning of the service out of reverence and expectation. But the choir director should not tell them to "hush"! He should instead lead them in joyous singing of praise to God.

PRAISE AND THANKSGIVING

What then *are* we to do in our silent prayers and in our quiet times? One means of developing a definition is to ascertain what a word is *not,* by contrasting it with another, similar term. Compare and contrast the two words "praise" and "thanksgiving." The former is an Old Testament word, and the latter is a New Testament term. The New Testament Scriptures regularly speak of thanksgiving that can be done in one's heart and in private, even "in a closet." But these passages are using Greek terms, not Hebrew. All of the Hebrew terms for praise, as we shall see, have about them a public and vocal nature. In contrast then, thanksgiving may be silent and private; praise is vocal and public. But both must be intense and genuine.

Westermann argues that all of the vocabulary of praise contains a public and vocal element. We find this factor especially in the vow of praise:

I will tell Your name to my brothers,
In the midst of the congregation I will praise You
(Ps. 22:22).

Westermann comments:

> This is a further reason why the translation "give thanks" is
> false here, for today no one considers this element to be a part
> of giving thanks. How different it would be, if everywhere,
> where in our translations of the Psalms we are called on to give
> thanks, the forensic element were also heard. Then it would be
> clear that this call, "give thanks . . . ," has been truly heard
> only by the one, who in addition to having a deep feeling of
> gratitude in his heart and to thanking God in private, also
> tells *in public* what God has done for him [his emphasis].[3]

Thanksgiving occurs when one breathes a prayer of thanks
to God for His mercy and goodness; *praise* occurs when one
tells someone else about it. Sometimes praise comes as the
response to answered prayer; at other times praise is the
result of meditation on the Scriptures that has led to a new
insight into the wonder of the Lord. Praise may come from an
ever-new sense of God's presence or a startling and dramatic
sense of one's dependence upon His goodness.

APPLES ON THE WINDSHIELD

Once I was driving home from a church some distance from
our home. I had just completed an exhilarating four-day
ministry. It was late at night, and I was quite sleepy. I had
been having allergy troubles and had taken a new allergy
medication, which made me drowsy. As I got near a highway
intersection in our rural area, suddenly I realized that I had

---

[3]Westermann, *Praise of God,* p. 30.

plowed straight through a red stop sign, where I should have made a right turn . . . *after* stopping. There was no continuation of my road straight ahead. It was a "T" intersection, and I was about to slam into a substantial post.

It would be difficult for me to tell you all of the thoughts that scrambled through my mind in that micro-second of awareness. My right leg was hurting, so taut was it as I shoved the brake pedal, it seemed, through the chassis. The post got nearer and nearer. My ears were only too well aware of the loud screeching sound. I kept thinking, *how in the world did I miss seeing the sign? Where did this post come from? Is this really the intersection? Are there any cars coming? Did the children milk the goat?*

Much more quickly than it takes to recount all of this, the incident was over. The car had stopped just inches from the post. The stop had been so sudden that things that had been on the back seat of the VW camper were on the floor in front of me. Included were two large boxes of apples. Some of the bruised fruit was still rolling. I was wringing wet, trembling and exhausted—and still unable to understand what drugged state had robbed me of my view of the sign.

What did I do? I prayed. I prayed for several minutes, conscious now of the many cars whizzing by behind me. I asked God to forgive me for my carelessness. I had endangered not only my own life but the lives of others as well. I also thanked God for life, for the fact that another car had not been there, that the brakes had held, that God was giving me another day.

Then, very slowly, I drove the rest of the way home. When I got inside, I found that I was still trembling. I told my wife, Beverly, what had happened, and I repeated to her my thanksgiving to God for life. In that context, praise occurred. For I then spoke out loud to another what earlier I had prayed to God. Praise occurred, for I was able to speak publicly my genuine expression of gratitude to my caring Father. In Westermann's words, I was one "who in addition to having a deep feeling of gratitude in his heart and to thanking God in private, also tells *in public* what God has done for him."[4] Praise is vocal, it is public, and it must be genuine. (By the way, the children *had* milked our goat!)

In this experience we lauded His name together. Together we participated in genuine worship, for we expressed our conviction of God's deliverance. When praise occurs, the community benefits. This is true whether the community is a family, a prayer group, or a congregation. This is the wonder of praise. True praise elevates God, not the speaker. True praise magnifies God in the community, not just in the thoughts of the one speaking. Praise is *constructive worship.* It should be a part of everyday living. *Praise is a matter of life and breath.* As long as the believer has life and breath, praise is due from his lips to our incomparable God.

NO THANKS!

One of the most startling and surprising observations of recent studies of the Book of Psalms is that in the Hebrew language there appears to be no word meaning "thank you." Modern Israeli Hebrew has taken a word from the Old Testament and now uses it for the meaning "thanks," but that word did not seem to mean "thanks" in the biblical period. This is hard for us to believe, so deeply ingrained in our culture is the word "to thank."[5]

It seems that the first word we wish to hear from our little children after "Mommy" and "Daddy" is "thank you." When our little Bruce was but two years old, he pronounced words that were new to him very distinctly and clearly. The words he had learned earlier, however, were still pronounced in his babyish approximation. It seemed that the "dit-du" that

[4]Ibid.

[5]This concept will be explained a bit more fully in the study of Psalm 138 in Part Two.

passed for "thank you" arose because he had learned it very early.

In many of our English versions of the Old Testament we find the words "thank," "thanks," and "thanksgiving." But these words are used in our English versions because of the necessary idiom of the target language; the precise meanings of the original words do not include the same range of meaning as our English word "thanks."

In the Old Testament culture, the word used in place of *thanks* was *praise*. That is, one would *tell another* what God had done, rather than merely saying, "Thank You, Lord." This factor may now be put in the context of the great words for praise that are found in the Psalms.

A LITTLE HEBREW

There are many words in the Old Testament vocabulary of praise. The words given in this section are Hebrew words that animate the Psalms.

Praise!

The word *hālal,* which is seen in the transliteration "Hallelujah!" ("Praise the Lord" or "Praise Yah!"), basically means "to be boastful," "to be excited in joy." This word is related to an Arabic word that was the shout of triumph at the end of a battle, when the soldier was alive, his army had won, and the booty was about to be divided.

Hālal is the Hebrew equivalent of whatever you say when you are watching a football game and your team has just scored the winning points. This word is what a nursing student says in coming out of an anatomy exam with an "A" grade, when she had struggled very hard to complete the course. This is the word of any experience calling for excited boasting or joyful expression. Our Psalms are replete with this word, but it is seen especially in the *Hālal* Psalms, beginning with Psalm 111.

Acknowledge in Public!

The Hebrew word *yādāh* is the term over which there is the controversy concerning the usual rendering "to thank." In the NASB translation of Psalm 138:1 we read:

> I will give Thee *thanks* with all my heart;
> I will sing praises to Thee before the gods.

As has been suggested above, the better rendering of this key verb is "to give public acknowledgment." For that reason, I suggest for this verse the following:

> I will give You *public acknowledgment* with all my heart;
> I will sing praises to You before the gods.

As was said above, one "gave thanks" to God in the Old Testament period by telling others what God had done. Praise is forensic.

Bless!

The verb *bārak* means "to bless." This is one of the most interesting verbs of the words for praise, for the question may be raised, "How can one bless God?" We may understand rather fully what is meant when we say that God has blessed us. He has saved us for all eternity. He has added us to the body of Christ. He has gifted us as His children. He has given to us ministries of various types to honor His name and to serve hurting people.

I appreciate readily the statement, "God has blessed me." But how may I bless *God?* Listen again to the familiar words of Psalm 103:1,2 for an answer:

> *Bless* Yahweh, O my soul;
> And all that is within me, *bless* His holy name.
> *Bless* Yahweh, O my soul,
> And forget none of His benefits.

An understanding of Hebrew parallelism, which was discussed in Chapter 4, explains the concept of "blessing God." The two members of the first verse are in *synonymous* parallelism. Both members speak of blessing God, and both describe this act as involving one's whole personality. The second verse is in *antithetical* parallelism; that is, the first line is affirmed by the denial of its opposite. Hence, "to bless" is "not to forget." Stated positively, "to bless" is "to remember." We *bless* God when we turn to Him and joyfully remember that He is the source of all that is good in our lives. The words of this Psalm develop the blessing of God in the verbs "pardons, heals, redeems, crowns, satisfies, and renews" (vv. 3–5). We *bless God* when we mark Him out as the source of all of our blessing.

Sing!

It should come as no surprise that many key words for praise in the Book of Psalms are musical terms. *Zāmar* is but one of these, having the idea "to make music in praise of God." This word is found, for example, in Psalm 92:1:

> It is good to give public acknowledgment to Yahweh,
> And to *sing praises* to Your name, O Most High!

Other important words for the singing of praise to Yahweh include *shîr,* "to sing," and *rānan,* "to sing for joy." The former is notable in Psalm 96:1:

> *Sing* to Yahweh a new song;
> *Sing* to Yahweh all the earth!

The other is used in Psalm 95:1:

> O come, let us *sing for joy* to Yahweh;
> Let us shout joyfully to the Rock of our salvation.

This same verb is translated as "shout for joy" in Psalm 145:7b. Many other terms for music are prominent in the Psalms.

In Old Testament life and culture, music was most prominent in the expressions of response given by the pious to the glory and goodness of the living God. In the history of the church this has been true as well. As I suggested earlier, a lack of prominence given to music may be a sad barometer of an unhealthy church.

Laud!

The shortest Psalm in the collection displays the Hebrew verb *shābaḥ*. Psalm 117:1 reads:

> Praise Yahweh, all nations;
> *Laud* Him, all peoples!

Often in English we limit the verb "to laud" to settings of funeral orations. This Psalm encourages, yes commands, all nations and all peoples to laud the ever-living Yahweh. "To laud" means "to speak well of." You can see at once how fitting this is as a term for praise. The same verb is found as well in Psalm 145:4a.

Shout in joy!

Perhaps the most foreign word for many of us in the vocabulary of praise in our somewhat restrained manner of worship is the word *rū(a)ʿ*. For this word means "to shout in joy." The Hebrew culture allowed for believers to get truly excited about the reality of their great God! We have already seen this verb in the second member of Psalm 95:1, "Let us *shout joyfully* to the Rock of our salvation." It is also used in Psalm 100:1:

> *Shout joyfully* to Yahweh, all the earth!

Some churches find this type of word to be very comfortable. I know of one church whose neighbors complain often because of the decibel level of the shouting in the praise of the Lord.

But not all people find this term to be congenial. When I was sharing the meaning of this word before students at the Alaska Bible College, I was asked how such terms would relate to the native peoples of Alaska. I was told that they are quite reserved by nature in their manner of expression. My feeling is that it is not necessary to expect peoples of various cultures to adopt in a wholesale way the culture of the Old Testament people to be truly biblical in praise. Nevertheless, the genuineness and the intensity suggested by verbs such as this may be expressed in a more reserved manner. If shouting is foreign to one's personality or culture, there ought to be at least the same *inner excitement* that can then lead to an *outward expression* legitimate to one's own situation (and neighbors!)

Proclaim!

One very wide-ranging word for speaking, calling, praying, preaching, and making proclamation is the Hebrew word *Qārā'*. This enters the vocabulary of praise at times in the Psalms. An example is seen in Psalm 116:17:

To You I shall offer a sacrifice of praise,[6]
And in the name Yahweh I will *make proclamation*.

Other verbs of speaking, saying, and telling become the words of praise at times. One fine example is the verb *nāgad*, "to declare," as in Psalm 92:2:

To declare Your loyal love in the morning,
And Your faithfulness by night.

[6]The Hebrew word here is *tôdāh*, a word related to *yādāh* (see p. 65).

Another similar word is *bāsar,* which means "to proclaim" and can mean "to proclaim the good news," that is, "to preach the gospel." It is best seen in Psalm 96:2,3:

> Sing to Yahweh, bless His name;
> *Proclaim good tidings* of His salvation from day to day.
> Tell of His glory among the nations,
> Among all the peoples [tell of] His wonderworks.

The first element of verse 3 uses another verb of speaking, *sāpar,* which is also found in Psalm 145:6b.

Extol!

(Some of my friends will wish me to state that this Hebrew word *rûm* is pronounced like our word "room" and not like the beverage made famous by pirates of yore.) The basic meaning of this verb is "to be high." In certain formations of the word it means "to extol." This word is thus a natural term for praise. God *is* high, and He is *made* high by our praise. Psalm 145:1 reads:

> I *extol* You, my God and King;
> And I will bless Your name for ever and ever![7]

These are some of the major terms in the vocabulary of praise. There are others, particularly musical terms and the common words for speaking. But the important observation we should make concerning this varied cluster of terms is the common denominator: *All are words of sound.* Praise in the Old Testament is vocal, public, and genuine. To repeat a comment about varying cultures: It is not necessary for all cultures to become Hebrew; but within each culture there should be the opportunity for the public expression of delight in the living God.

---

[7]Other rarer words expressive of the praise of God are found in this Psalm. One is *śi(a)ḥ,* "to speak thoughtfully" (v. 5b), and another is *nābaᶜ,* "to bubble (with praise)" (v. 7a).

PRAISE HIM IN THE CONGREGATION

God should be praised by His people at all times and in all circumstances of our living. But the most natural forum for praise is in the congregation at worship. Repeatedly in the Psalms, we read of the desire of the saints to praise God when in the assembly of the righteous. Psalm 149:1, for example, reads,

> Hallelujah!
> Sing to Yahweh a new song,
> And His praise in the congregation of the faithful.

It is in the congregation of believers that praise most naturally should occur.

Those who are unable to join the congregation in praise feel the loss most deeply. The lament from the sons of Korah pictures this distress in long-cherished words:

> As the deer pants for the water brooks,
> So I pant for You, O God (Ps. 42:1).

These words were brought about by one who was in a distant land, but who one day hoped again to join the congregation in the praise of God (see Ps. 42:11).

As a thirsty deer longs for refreshment at a mountain brook, so the believer should have an insatiable desire to worship God in the setting of the community.

And yet, sadly, it seems that one thing done rather poorly today in many evangelical churches is just this: How rarely do we really worship! We gather, we listen to sermons, we participate in the activities of the church; but rarely do we seem to go to church principally to worship God.

Think again through the vocabulary of praise in this chapter:

> Be excitedly boastful!
> Acknowledge in public!

Bless; mark Him out as the source of blessing!
Sing praises and make music!
Laud; speak well of Him!
Shout joyfully!
Make proclamation!
Extol, speak thoughtfully, "bubble" with praise!

There *are* times to be silent before the Lord, both as an individual and in the congregation. Sometimes our silence before Him may be an expression of our trust. Psalm 131 pictures this trusting silence beautifully:

My heart is not proud, O LORD,
   my eyes are not haughty;
I do not concern myself with great matters
   or things too wonderful for me.
But I have stilled and quieted my soul;
   like a weaned child with its mother,
   like a weaned child is my soul within me.

O Israel, put your hope in the LORD
   both now and forevermore (Ps. 131:1–3 NIV).

But praise is not a time for silence; it is a time for sound. The sound is not to be just noise, but words—words of adoration of the God of glory. On one occasion when he had become a fugitive from the sanctuary, David thought back in longing to the joyful times of praising God in the community. He also looked forward in hope to new opportunities to praise God. Here are his words:

I have seen you in the sanctuary
   and beheld your power and your glory.
Because your love is better than life,
   my lips will glorify you.
I will praise you as long as I live,
   and in your name I will lift up my hands.

71

My soul will be satisfied as with the richest of foods;
with singing lips my mouth will praise you (Ps. 63:2–5
NIV).

The praise of God is the central issue of the Book of Psalms.
Along with our rightful emphases on preaching and praying,
there should be a corresponding emphasis on *participation* in
the worship of God in our services. We need opportunities to
minister to each other in praise, to share with those who will
understand best our excited boastings in the wonder of knowing the living God. We need to be strengthened by each other
in the delight we have in the risen Christ. We need to use our
lips to glorify Him.

CHAPTER 6

Praise on Target

Praise may be given in many and varied circumstances, from a social gathering to the congregation at worship. But the one we must praise is God. *In the Book of Psalms praise is always directed to God.* That is the only way praise may be said to be on target. This might seem to be obvious, but it must be given emphasis for it is so very crucial. Praise is not merely feeling good inside. Praise is not just a sense of belonging in the community. Praise is rather participation in the *worship of God.* It is the expression of delight in knowing Him and in learning more about the Savior. Praise *happens* when God is glorified.[1]

In the Book of Psalms we find that there are two principal ways in which praise is "on target" as it is directed toward God. We praise Him for *who He is,* and we praise Him for *what He does.* As we have observed in an earlier chapter, these two expressions of praise lead to two categories of hymns in the Bible. God is praised for who He is in the Psalms of Descriptive Praise and for what He does in the Psalms of Declarative Praise.

[1]As the Nicene Creed states, "We believe in One God the Father Almighty . . . and in one Lord Jesus Christ, the only begotten Son of God . . . of one substance with the Father . . . and in the Holy Spirit, the Lord and Giver of life, who proceeds from the Father. . . ." Thus I confess three divine Persons (Father, Son, and Holy Spirit) in one undivided nature. When I speak of God, or the Lord, or Yahweh, as "He" or "Him," as revealed in the Psalms, I will ordinarily be referring to God the Father, unless I specifically note otherwise.

WHO HE IS

If we think about it, we should agree that there could be no more exciting study, no more rewarding task, than to learn more concerning the God we worship.

Yet many Christian people are not excited at all about the study of God. Perhaps part of the problem lies in the fact that some Christians have left this study to the "experts." It may even be true that some of the "experts" are content with this state of affairs. Yet the study of God should be the interest of all of His people. How shall we ever praise Him rightly unless we know Him well?

The study of God is termed *theology*. But this term is used in schools to describe the whole range of topics related to God and man, life and death, origins and consummations, angels and demons, sin and redemption. Principally, though, the word "theology" speaks of the *knowledge of God*. It is theology in this narrow sense that I wish to stress in this section.

We find in the Book of Psalms that God is praised for *who He is* along three lines. (1) Praise is directed toward God on the basis of His attributes; (2) praise is directed toward God centered in His name; and (3) praise is directed toward God as expressed in His incomparability. These are the factors that animate the Psalms of Descriptive Praise. Later in the chapter, we shall balance these elements by turning to the praise of God in terms of *what He does* in the Psalms of Declarative Praise.

PRAISE GOD FOR HIS ATTRIBUTES!

The attributes of God are the ways in which God displays His nature. These are the ways in which God causes Himself to be known by His people. Every parent is asked by a little child, "What is God like?" Perhaps it is only when asked that question by a little one that we really begin to ask it ourselves. We learn what God is like by looking at the way in which He reveals Himself. And these attributes which are then displayed become great targets for the praise of God the Father, the Son, and the Holy Spirit.

It will not be my purpose to list all of the divine attributes that capture the imagination of the psalmists and toward which they direct their joyful praise. I wish merely to list some of the more prominent attributes of God in the praise of the Psalms to set the stage for our further enjoyment of these hymns and to give us a basis for our own praise of the triune God.

God is great! We live in an age of super heroes and advertising hype. The word "great" may have become somewhat devalued in our thinking because of overuse. It seems that every new cereal, soap, or deodorant is called "great." But when the word "great" is used of God, this somewhat relative word becomes infinite. Who can be greater than our great God? Psalm 86:10a exults: "For *great* are You!" Psalm 145:3 rejoices:

Great is Yahweh, and highly to be praised;
And His *greatness* is unsearchable.

God shows loyal love! If any one single term describing the character of God in His sublime attributes were to be made central in the Psalms, I believe it would be the Hebrew word *ḥesed*. This is a word so rich in its meaning that translators vie with each other in thinking up new ways to render its riches. Some of the many translations are *mercy, merciful goodness, lovingkindness, merciful kindness,* and the like. The major dictionaries for Hebrew study go two directions in their meanings for this word. One of these dictionaries emphasizes the dimension of *loyalty* as the basic meaning of the word; the other dictionary stresses the concept of *mercy* or *love.*

A growing number of Old Testament scholars believe that this word is basically two-dimensional. Hence, the most satisfactory rendering will show both aspects. I prefer the translation "loyal love." The RSV renders *ḥesed* nicely by "steadfast love." In some contexts the aspect of love is prominent. In others the aspect of loyalty is stressed. In those passages where loyalty should be given its due, perhaps the better translation would be "loving loyalty."

The word *ḥesed* is found throughout the Psalter. One Psalm has this word in every single verse. Psalm 136 is designed for antiphonal choirs. One choir gives a summons to praise or a predication of praise, and the other choir responds twenty-six times: "For His *loyal love* is everlasting."[2]

God is holy! Many scholars believe that God's preeminent attribute is His holiness. Whether we should think of the attributes of God in levels of importance may be debated. There is no question, however, that the poets and prophets of the Bible regularly stress the holiness of God.

The Hebrew word translated "holy" basically means "set apart, distinct, different, removed from." The holiness of Yahweh of Hosts is the subject of seraphic praise in the great throne vision of Isaiah (Is. 6:3). The Book of Leviticus has as its ongoing theme, "I Yahweh am holy" (see, e.g., Lev. 11:45).

Within the Psalter, God's holiness is significantly praised. Psalm 99, for example, has a threefold *holy* that corresponds to the threefold *holy* of the seraphs of Isaiah 6. In this Psalm verse 3 reads, "Holy is He." Verse 5 reads, "Holy is He." And the climax is found in verse 9, "For *holy* is Yahweh our God!"

God is good! That God is good is not a mere truism. It is in fact one of the most happy declarations of the Psalms. What if the god with whom we had to do were evil? But praise His

[2]In Part Two there is a development of Psalm 13 in which *ḥesed* is most prominent.

name, He is good! Such is regularly and boastfully affirmed in the Psalms. Often the goodness of God is coupled to His *ḥesed*, His loyal love. Such is the case in Psalm 107:1:

> Give public acknowledgment to Yahweh for He is *good;*
> For His loyal love is everlasting!

God is righteous! The righteousness of God is a major affirmation of the Psalter. That is, He conforms to the standards of His own perfection. To be righteous is to conform to a standard, as Israel was commanded to do with respect to weights and measures. The tradesmen of Israel were not to have two sets of weights, one for purchasing and another for selling (see Lev. 19:36). There was to be one standard for weights and measures, and the merchants were to have weights that conformed to the standard. The word "righteous" defines this concept. One text affirming the righteousness of Yahweh is Psalm 119:137:

> *Righteous* are You, O Yahweh,
> And upright are Your judgments.

That God is righteous and yet justifies the sinner is the background of the gospel. That God is righteous and judges the unrepentant is the foundation of the wrath of God. So it is that the righteousness of God underlies both His grace to the pious and His anger toward the wicked in such passages as Psalm 14. Verse 5 describes the terrible dread of the wicked when they one day stand before the throne of the God they have ignored or opposed through this life:

> There they will be in excruciating dread,
> For God is in the righteous generation.

Verse 7 describes the delight of God's people as they pray for the restitution of righteousness to be evidenced in the salvation He will bring:

O that the salvation of Israel were come from Zion,
When Yahweh restores the fortunes of His people;
   Jacob will rejoice, Israel will be glad!

God is truth! Another major declaration of the splendors of
Yahweh's character is "truth." God is truth. This facet of His
perfections is praised in Psalm 138:2ab:

I will bow down toward Your holy temple,
And give public acknowledgment to Your name
   for Your loyal love and Your *truth*.[3]

The word "truth" has to do with God's abiding faithfulness,
enduring steadfastness—His *certain* character. Not only is
God truth, but so are the Scriptures that come from Him. The
Scriptures of God are the adequate expression of His character, as they correspond to His essential truthfulness.[4]

God has great glory! At least one more attribute of God
praised in the Psalms should be mentioned. This is His *glory*.
The word "glory" forms one of the great shouts of praise in the
Psalms. In Psalm 138:5 we read:

And they will sing of the ways of Yahweh,
For great is the *glory* of Yahweh.

In one sense God's glory is a summary of His attributes. His
glory relates to the expression of His character, His royal

[3]There is a study of this text in context in Part Two. The following colon is
most difficult: "For You have magnified Your word above all Your name."
[4]This is an emphasis that will be made in the study of Psalm 19 in Part
Two. In a booklet on the nature of the Scriptures, Charles C. Ryrie has
written, "We believe God's Word to be infallible simply because God Himself
is infallible. God is true (John 3:33; 17:3; Rom. 3:4; 1 Thess. 1:9), and this true
God speaks in the true Scriptures." *We Believe in Biblical Inerrancy* (Kansas
City, Kan.: Walterick Publishers, 1972), p. 8.

nature, His divine essence. R. T. France writes, "The unapproachable majesty and dazzling brightness of God marks Him out as 'the King of glory' (Ps. 24:7–10)."[5]

In any listing of the attributes of God that call for praise in the Psalms, there is bound to be a difficulty because of omissions. God is not to be limited to the above listed perfections. But these splendors are representative of those factors of His character that regularly call for praise in the Book of Psalms. God is worthy of the excitement of His people.

GOD'S ATTRIBUTES

If we think rightly about God, we cannot view His perfections as though they were abstractions, merely topics for discussion (or debate!). The Bible reveals the nature of God *as He relates to His people*. We are to be excited about the fact that God is good, because He is good to us. We are to praise God for His loyal love, because He has demonstrated His loyal love to us.

One of the Psalms of consummate artistry and strong emotion that develops the attributes of God as the focus of praise is Psalm 139. This Psalm renders praise to God for His *active relationship* to the believer. Psalm 139 stresses God's transcendence and majesty, but in a way that leads us not to discussion but to praise: "What a great God we have!"

In this Psalm the believer rejoices that God knows him in a way that is full of wonder (vv. 1–6). He delights in the knowledge that God is present with him wherever he might be (vv. 7–12). He acknowledges that God has formed him with wonder and skill (vv. 13–16). He stands in awe of the thoughts of God that are beyond the believer's comprehension (vv. 17,18). He finds himself at odds with all who are enemies of God (vv.

[5]R.T. France, *The Living God* (Downers Grove, Ill.: Inter-Varsity, 1970), p. 66.

19,22). And the believer desires to be attuned to the character of God (vv. 23,24).[6]

In reading Psalm 139 we cannot but exult in praise to God for the way in which His perfections are expressed in active relationship to His people.

GOD IN FOCUS

Nothing can be more important in our lives than a right and proper view of God. By learning what God is like, we are prepared to live for the praise of His glory. A missionary friend of mine, who works among the native peoples of Canada, has done a good deal of thinking concerning the attributes of God. He has attempted to think of an attribute for each of the letters of the English alphabet (and he says that he lacks an attribute for only one letter!).

As he faces new issues or problems in daily living he relates them to the character of God. Often he does this by means of an acrostic based on a key word to direct his attention to several of God's perfections. For example, he might use the word "focus" with the idea of bringing his problem into focus by means of the character of God. So the first letter might speak of God's *f*aithfulness, the second of His *o*mniscience, the third of His *c*reativeness, the next of His *u*nderstanding, and the last of His *s*overeignty. By *focusing* on God's character through this acrostic, this missionary is better prepared to face that new problem in his life. Moreover, he is better prepared to give praise to God for being the God He has shown Himself to be.

LAUGHING WITH SARAH

It is hard to overemphasize the importance of the name of God in the theology of the Old Testament. The preeminent

[6]I have developed this Psalm in a brochure on the abortion question entitled *In Celebrating Love of Life* (Portland: Western Baptist Press, 1977).

name for God in the Hebrew Bible is Yahweh. This great name, which was formerly rendered Jehovah by many,[7] is the convenient summary of God's perfections.

In the culture of the Old Testament, a name was often used as a summary of character, a description of personality. The name *Isaac* serves as a splendid example. During the seemingly interminable period of waiting for his birth, both of his parents had moments of laughing at the promise of God. At one point when the covenant promise was being renewed by God, Abraham "fell on his face and laughed" (Gen. 17:17) at the thought of his becoming a father at the age of one hundred and his wife's becoming a mother at the age of ninety.

Shortly following that incident, Sarah also laughed as the promise of a son was repeated by the Lord through Abraham's three visitors at the oaks of Mamre. When accused of laughing, she denied this out of fear. But the response from God was, "No, but you did laugh" (Gen. 18:15).

Finally the child was born. God kept His word; He did just as He had promised (see Gen. 21:1,2). The child was given the name *Isaac*. In Hebrew this name means "He laughs." This word is a gloriously happy name that suggests the joy of the aged parents as the old hope for a son was finally realized. In a culture when far more meaning than today was attached to the birth of a son, Isaac's birth brought laughter into the home. His name also causes us to recall the laughing of another sort done by both of his parents in the years of their longing. The name suggests that in the birth of this son, God Himself is getting the last laugh! If so, it is a last laugh of joy and not rebuff.

Sarah rightly theologized on the meaning of her son's name in these words: "God has made laughter for me; everyone who hears will laugh with me" (Gen. 21:6). In the name *Isaac* God is laughing. In the same name Sarah and Abraham learned to

[7]I have discussed this issue in my article, "What Is in a Name?" in William F. Kerr, *God: What Is He Like?* (Wheaton, Ill.: Tyndale, 1977).

laugh in a new way. We hear the name, and we get the joke as
well; and we join in their happy laughter.

PRAISE GOD FOR HIS NAME!

What is in a name? In the culture of the Old Testament a
great deal was in a name. And if the name is the name of God,
then everything is in that name. The name *Yahweh* speaks of
God's eternal existence. But it says more than just that God
exists. The name is dynamic in its meaning. *Yahweh* speaks
of God's existence for the good of His people. The name is a
name of relationship, of covenant, of promise. By the name
Yahweh, God is asserting by His eternal character that He
will forever relate to His people.

There is a sense in which all of the biblical theology of the
Old Testament might be reduced to the meaning of the name
of God. The Old Testament is basically a book about the
nature and work of God. The name Yahweh points to both His
person and His work in a way that calls for praise.

From the word *Hallelujah,* which means "Praise
Yah(weh)," to the more extended commands for praise, the
name of God is a consistent target for our praise. Psalm
113:1b commands: "Praise the name Yahweh!"

To repeat, the name of God is a convenient summary of all
of the splendors of God. We praise His name whenever we
praise God for His being, for His character, or for His attributes. His name *must* be praised. His name *will* be praised.

The wonder is that His name *may be praised by us.*

THERE IS NONE LIKE HIM

Sometimes we say of someone, with a sigh of relief, that "he
is one of a kind" or "there is no one like her." Yet at other
times we say similar words about someone, but with some

regret, wishing there were others like him or her. But when we say of God that there is no one like Him, we do so with great joy, not with relief or regret. The theological term for this concept is that God is *incomparable*. That is, He is beyond all points of reference.

Since we learn by making comparisons, the unknown with the known, it is hard for us to think in terms of the incomparable. It is natural for us to make comparisons.

The mayor of a large West Coast city demonstrated this. She found herself at a concert where she had an official function to perform, but then left soon after the music began. She was rather unimpressed by what little she had heard— the artistry of one of the world's greatest musicians, Andrés Segovia. When the mayor was asked by a reporter what she thought of the music, she said, "I realize he is supposed to have this marvelous technique, but as far as I could tell, he sounded to me about the same as my children did when they were first learning to play the guitar."

Gasp! Comparing the "incomparable" Segovia's performance to her children's twangings while learning the guitar is somewhat akin to comparing a symphony by Beethoven to "The Farmer in the Dell."

The mayor erred. But we also err if we use the word "incomparable" in an absolute sense when referring to any mortal. Segovia may be regarded by one critic as beyond comparison. But there are other great guitarists, each with his own champions. For Segovia, the word "incomparable" is a term of honor only.

When we think of God, however, we are instructed to think of Him as the *(absolutely) incomparable* One.[8] There is none to be compared to God. No person and no thing may be even a frame of reference. His thoughts transcend our thoughts and His ways our ways.

---

[8]Strictly speaking, of course, the term *incomparable* should have no modifier. Advertising hype and careless usage have teamed together to cheapen great words such as this.

A MULTITUDE OF ZEROS

Knowing that there is none to be compared with the living Yahweh is a major subject of praise in the Book of Psalms. Living in a world in which the nations round about believed in many gods, the psalmists might have said merely that the God of Israel is better than the god of Moab or superior to the god of Babylon. However, rejecting all other gods as idols, the poets of Israel shouted: "Who is like Yahweh our God?" (Ps. 113:5a).

On occasion, for the sake of argument, there may be a comparison made with pagan deities. In Psalm 96:4 there is this comparative statement made:

> For great is Yahweh, and greatly to be praised;
> He is to be feared above all gods.

In this verse there seems to be the concession that there are other gods, but that the God of Israel is superior. The next verse shatters this impression with a pun:

> For all the gods of the peoples are *idols,*
> But Yahweh has made the heavens (Ps. 96:5).

In these words there is a double play on words. In the first level of meaning we see the contrast between worshiping a created thing (an idol) as against worshiping the Creator of all the universe (Yahweh). The second level of the pun is seen in the meaning of the Hebrew word translated "idols." This word is an intensive plural of the Hebrew word for "nothing." That is, to worship an alternative to God is to worship less than nothing! Yahweh is incomparable. All alternatives make a multitude of zeros.[9]

[9]The Hebrew word for "idols" is *'elîlîm,* an intensive plural of "nothing"; it means "nothingnesses." It sounds very much like the word for God which is *'elôhîm.* This latter word is an intensive plural of the root idea of "might, strength"; it means "the most mighty." This is a devastating pun on idols.

WHAT HE DOES

As we have seen, praise is given to God for who He is and for what He does. In the Declarative Psalms of praise, the psalmists exult in the actions of God, in His mighty deeds, in His wonderful works. These Psalms praise God for His relatedness to His creation and His aid to His people. The works that call for praise in these Psalms include all of God's acts from creation past to the consummation of the ages in the future rule of God on the earth. Salvation, redemption, response to prayer, providence, protection, guidance, healing, sustaining, forgiving, crowning, satisfying—these are just a few of the actions that call for praise in the Book of Psalms.

One of the actions of God that should be cited is *His constant care* of His people. Psalm 121 assures the believer that the Creator of the cosmos is his constant companion, protecting and caring for him along his daily path. The One who cares for the faithful never relaxes His watchfulness. He never forgets His concern:

> Yahweh will keep your going out and your coming in
> From this time forth and forever (Ps. 121:8).

Another of the great actions of God is that *He speaks,* and His words may be trusted as they reflect His character. In the midst of a very hostile world, in which the words of the wicked are a constant source of complaint and distress, David delights in the words of God that comfort, help, and are true:

> The words of Yahweh are pure words;
> As silver tried in a furnace on the earth,
>   refined seven times (Ps. 12:6).

Yet another of the mighty works of Yahweh is *His provision in nature.* Psalm 135 speaks of rain as the gift of God that flows from His greatness, His will, and His treasuries:

For I know that Yahweh is great,
And that our Lord is above all gods.
All which Yahweh delights, He does,
In heaven and in earth,
In the seas and in all deeps.
He is the one who causes vapors to ascend from the ends
  of the earth;
Who makes lightnings for the rain;
Who brings forth wind from His treasuries (Ps. 135:5–7).

These and innumerable other actions call for praise to His name from the hymnists of ancient Israel. Psalm 92:5 declares:

How great are Your works, O Yahweh!
Your thoughts are very deep.

LET US THEN PRAISE HIM!

The Book of Psalms centers on the praise of God. Praise of God is on target when we praise Him for who He is and for what He does. Praise is the great privilege of the life and breath of faith.

Perhaps the best way to conclude this chapter is to read one of the Psalms of praise, Psalm 145, and to share its experience of genuine, vocal, and public declaration of the exceeding excellence of our incomparable God.

Many of the words for praise that were discussed in the last chapter will be found in this Psalm. Read through the Psalm, and see how many of these words for praise you can find. Also, many of the concepts of the present chapter are found here. As you read, ask yourself what is said in praise of God for who He is. Ask as well what is said in praise of God for what He does. See how these elements are balanced in this Psalm and how they interplay with each other.

One element of this Psalm that will not be evident from the English translation is that it is an acrostic. In this poem the poet has begun by writing the letters of the Hebrew alphabet down the side of the page. He has then written his poem so that the first word of the first verse begins with the first letter of the alphabet, and the first word of the second verse begins with the second letter of the alphabet. One might think that this procedure would lead to a lifeless and mechanical approach to poetry. But the poets of the Old Testament were well adapted to this technique. They seemed to do it for the enjoyment of the task as well, perhaps, as to encourage the memorization of the poem.

AN ALPHABET OF PRAISE
Psalm 145

(1) I extol You, My God, O King,   *Aleph*
And I will bless Your name for ever and ever.

(2) In every day I will bless You,   *Beth*
And I will praise Your name for ever and ever.

(3) Great is Yahweh and greatly to be praised,   *Gimel*
And concerning His greatness there is no searching out.

(4) Generation to generation will laud Your works,   *Daleth*
And Your mighty acts they will declare.

(5) The splendid glory of Your majesty.   *He*
And the words of Your wonders I will speak thoughtfully.

(6) And the strength of Your awesome deeds they   *Waw*
will speak,
And Your greatness I will assuredly proclaim.

(7) The memory of Your great goodness they will   *Zayin*
bubble,
And Your righteousness they will proclaim in shouts of joy.

PRAISE! A MATTER OF LIFE AND BREATH

(8) Graciously compassionate is Yahweh,   *Heth*
    Slow of anger but great of loyal love.

(9) The goodness of Yahweh is for all,   *Teth*
    And His loving compassion is over all His works.

(10) All Your works give public acknowledgment to   *Yod*
     You, O Yahweh,
     And Your saints bless You.

(11) Of the glory of Your kingdom they speak,   *Kaph*
     And Your power they declare.

(12) To make known to mankind His mighty acts,   *Lamedh*
     And the glorious majesty of His kingdom.

(13) Your kingdom is an everlasting kingdom,   *Mem*
     And Your dominion endures throughout all gen-
     erations.[10]

(14) Yahweh supports all who fall,   *Samekh*
     And raises up all who are bowed down.

(15) The eyes of all wait upon You,   *Ayin*
     And You are giving them their food in its time.

(16) You open Your hand,   *Pe*
     And You satisfy for all living their desire.

(17) Righteous is Yahweh in all His ways,   *Tsadhe*
     And faithful in all His works.

[10]The verse for the Hebrew letter *Nun* is lacking in the Hebrew Bibles we have today. It is found in the Greek translation of the Bible (the Septuagint) as follows:

(13a) Reliable is Yahweh in all His ways,
      And faithful in all His works.

The names of the letters of the Hebrew alphabet are found to the right of the verses. Readers of the English Bible will find these letters in Psalm 119. That Psalm is a most ambitious acrostic, having eight verses for each letter of the Hebrew alphabet. In most English Bibles each section of eight verses is printed with the Hebrew letter and name in the headings.

(18) Near is Yahweh to all who call upon Him   *Qoph*
      To all who call on Him in truth.

(19) The desire of those who fear Him He will do,   *Resh*
      And their cry He will hear and He will save them.

(20) Yahweh preserves all who love Him,   *Sin/Shin*
      But all the wicked He will exterminate.

(21) May my mouth speak the praise of Yahweh,   *Taw*
      And may all flesh bless His holy name for ever
       and ever!

In the alphabet of praise we see again that God is to be praised for who He is and for what He does. The center of the Book of Psalms is the praise of the incomparable Yahweh by His people. Plan now to add your words of praise to His name today. Perhaps it may be in an informal setting. Possibly you may do this in a church service where people are asked to share God's goodness. Pray about it. Plan for it. Then praise God for who He is. Praise Him for what He does. Let your praise be "on target." Let your *life and breath* count for His glory.

CHAPTER 7

How Did We Get the Psalms?

How *did* we get the Psalms? This question cannot be asked in isolation. It has to be asked in the context of the larger question, how did we get the Bible?

GOD IN A HELICOPTER

The earliest memory I have of learning something about the Bible was one Christmas when I was three or four years old. My parents were not Christians at the time, but they did say something about the story of Jesus' birth. They told me that this was written in the Bible. When I asked where the Bible came from, they told me it came from God.

I knew that Santa brought gifts in his reindeer-drawn sleigh. Somehow I imagined that God dropped the Bible to earth from a helicopter! I had an imaginary playmate during those years who regularly came to my backyard in a 'copter. God, I supposed, must travel about something like my friend "the Gook."

When God dropped this Bible down, I understood it to be complete, in English, with a synthetic leather cover, and the words of Jesus in red.

Many Christians today no longer talk of Santa Claus, perhaps never had an imaginary playmate, and certainly do not picture God in a helicopter. But in saying that "the Bible came from God," they still imply something not too very far removed from my childish, imaginary picture. Saying "the Bible came from God" seems to say it all.

Or does it?

THE DUAL AUTHORSHIP OF SCRIPTURE

With the orthodox of all ages and all communions, we happily affirm the supernatural inspiration of the documents of the Bible. We believe that the Scriptures of God are inspired or God-breathed in the fullest sense of the term. We have learned from the teaching of Paul:

> All Scripture is inspired by God and profitable for teaching, for reproof, for correction, for training in righteousness; that the man of God may be adequate, equipped for every good work (2 Tim. 3:16,17 NASB).

We have also learned from Peter:

> But know this first of all, that no prophecy of Scripture is a matter of one's own interpretation, for no prophecy was ever made by an act of human will, but men moved by the Holy Spirit spoke from God (2 Pet. 1:20,21 NASB).

The first passage emphasizes the ultimate source of Scripture, the "out-breathing" of God. The second text speaks of the human role in the inspiration process as that of an agent, not as an initiator; the writers of the Bible were blown along by the breath of God, as are sails by the driving wind.

Any approach to the Scriptures that does not begin with these fundamental affirmations is likely to err greatly in its estimation of the nature of the Bible. At the same time, it is evident that the Scriptures are most complex in their origin, for the dual nature of their source is unique among all literatures of human history.

The orthodox understanding of the phenomenon of inspired

Scripture has been that the Scriptures may be said to have had *dual authorship;* they are the product of God and man. But the nature of this dual authorship is difficult to understand and more difficult to state with precision. The dual nature of the writing of Scripture is *not* that of *collaboration,* as two human authors might collaborate in the writing of a biology textbook or a cookbook. Further, the many varieties of literature within the Old Testament especially demand a multiplex explanation.

THE PROPHETS AND REVELATION

We may use the word "revelation" in two ways. Used broadly, "revelation" refers to the whole of Scripture as a synonym for "inspiration." Thus we may affirm without hesitation that the whole of Scripture is revelation. But in a more narrow use of the word, "revelation" may be used to mean certain parts of the inspired Bible. In this more restrictive concept, "revelation" speaks of those parts of the fully inspired Scriptures in which God communicates new knowledge through His messengers. Lewis Sperry Chafer wrote, "In its theological usage, the term *revelation* is restricted to the divine act of communicating to man what otherwise man would not know."[1]

With this more restrictive use of "revelation" in mind, it is possible to say that all Scripture is inspired, but not all Scripture is revelation. All Scripture is the "out-breathing" of God, but not all Scripture is the making known of that which otherwise could not be known, as "revelation" is here understood to mean. *Revelation* is God's disclosure of Himself and His will. *Inspiration* is the broader term that governs the entirety of the Scriptures.

[1] Lewis Sperry Chafer, *Systematic Theology,* 8 vols. (Dallas: Dallas Theological Seminary, 1947), vol. 1, p. 48.

The *prophets* were the *spokesmen* for Yahweh.[2] They were the primary agents for the revelation of God and His will. In Jeremiah's inaugural vision we have one of the most descriptive illustrations of the relationship between God and His spokesmen in the process of revelation. Jeremiah, like Moses (see Ex. 4:10–17), was also reluctant to be God's prophet, even though God had designed him as His prophet before his embryo ever began to take form in his mother's womb (see Jer. 1:5). One of Jeremiah's reasons for hesitation was his own sense of personal inadequacy respecting his speaking ability (see v. 6). To meet this disclaimer of the reluctant prophet, God graphically and visually impressed him with the real nature of his task:

> Then Yahweh stretched out His hand and touched my
>   mouth,
> And Yahweh said to me,
>   "Behold, I have put My words in your mouth" (v. 9).

Here we have one of the most insightful explanations of the dual nature of the origin of Scripture in the entire Bible. The hand of God touching the mouth of the prophet-elect, as it were, put God's words in the man's mouth. The words were God's; the mouth was Jeremiah's. God "out-breathed" the words; Jeremiah spoke them. God moved the man by the Holy Spirit; Jeremiah spoke from God. The origin in God assures us of the integrity of the message. The transmission through the mouth of the man allows for the creative shaping of the

[2]The Hebrew word for "prophet" *(nābî')* is still debated by scholars, but likely means "one called" by its etymology and "one who speaks for another" by its usage in the Old Testament. A study of the call of Moses displays the significance of this word as "spokesman" (see Ex. 4:10–17, particularly v. 16; and Ex. 7:1-2, "Then Yahweh said to Moses, 'See, I make you as God to Pharaoh, and your brother Aaron shall be your *prophet.* You shall speak all that I command you, and your brother Aaron shall speak to Pharaoh that he let the sons of Israel go out of his land.' "

words of God in literature consequent with the man's native gifts and his personality. God's words in the mouth of Jeremiah sound different from God's words in the mouth of Isaiah. In both cases the words are God's, but the mouths are those of the prophets.

This model of the dual nature of the Scriptures does not mean, as some critics have assumed, that the (presumably) perfect words of God will (naturally) become somewhat tarnished as they are transmitted through the personalities of (admittedly) sinful men. My own study of the wicked prophet Balaam (see Num. 22–25)[3] presents the case that God's Word is not corrupted by a sinful agent. Balaam fought against the intent of God's Word. He wished to curse Israel, but he had to bless Israel. He himself had to acknowledge:

"God is not a man that He is able to lie,
Nor a son of man that He is able to repent;
Has He said, and will He not do it?
Or has He spoken, and will He not accomplish it?
Behold, I have received a commandment to bless;
When He has blessed, then I am not able to revoke it"
(Num. 23:19,20).

Revelation, then, is essentially the function of the prophet as he channels the words of God to the people. In transmitting those words, he gives them shape with his own creativity, personality, and art; but he transmits them *faithfully,* for they are the words of God in him. He can do no other.

THE PSALMISTS AND THEIR RESPONSES

Now if we redirect our attention from the prophetic literature to the Book of Psalms, we sense that here we are often

[3]"The Theology of the Balaam Oracles: A Pagan Diviner and the Word of God" (Unpublished Th.D. dissertation; Dallas Theological Seminary, 1973); also see Charles Lee Feinberg *Festschrift,* ed. Paul Feinberg and John Feinberg (Chicago: Moody, forthcoming).

dealing with something a bit different from the words of the prophets. The Psalms generally do not center on new revelation, but rather on *responses* to earlier revelation. That is, the Psalms basically are the expressions of the believer who has heard the sure prophetic Word of God but who lives in the troubled cauldron of society. His responses are often twofold: God is great, but life is tough! Hence, we have the two major categories of Psalms, which we noted earlier: the Psalms of praise and the Psalms of lament. The basic thrust of the Psalms is that of *response*.[4]

It would be a mistake to press this distinction too far, of course. For in fact there are many Psalms in which there *are* new revelations, and there are several Psalms in which there are specific predictive prophecies.[5] Yet viewed broadly, it is the primary function of the Psalms to respond to God, not to reveal new truth. It is quite important to assert at this point that the responses of the Psalms are *inspired;* they are in accord with reality, and they are consequent with truth in God.

THE WISE AND REFLECTION

Were we then to move to the *wisdom* literature, a third main body of literature within the Old Testament, we would find yet another distinction. The wisdom material is not basically new revelation, nor is this literature mainly the language of response. In the wisdom literature we come to the language of *reflection*. A picture we may have in our minds as we read the Book of Proverbs is that of an aged man, the sage, with a group of young men at his feet. They are his pupils, but he tenderly and paternally calls them his "sons." They are indentured to him for instruction in wisdom. It is also possi-

---

[4]Westermann speaks of the Psalms as "an occurrence from man to God," *Praise of God,* p. 154.

[5]See, for example, the study of Psalm 65, in Chapter 13.

ble that the sage—in concert with his wife (see, e.g., Prov. 6:20)—was instructing his own sons to follow in his steps of training as royal courtiers. Whether indentured or genetic, his sons sit at his feet to listen to the wisdom he has gained.

The wisdom that the wise man shares with his sons has been acquired over a lifetime. He has listened to the words of the prophets. He has joined in the hymns of praise written by the psalmists. But he has also been a keen student of nature, human personalities, and God's ways in providence. He does not communicate new revelation primarily, but reflection on the ways in which God's world works.

The wise man has also listened to the words of the wise men of many other lands. Believing that all truth is God's truth, he has tested the wisdom of the sages from other lands against truth as he knows it. He has sifted these sayings, as it were, through a grid of faith in Yahweh, the only God of reality. Those things that he believes to be in accord with truth, reality, and God, he has assimilated into his own manner of expression. It is not surprising to find, then, that many of the sayings in the Book of Proverbs are common with wisdom sentiments found in Egyptian literature as well as in other national collections.[6]

The main message of the wisdom writers is submission to the authority and majesty of Yahweh. The term that these writers use for this submission is "fear" in the expression, "the fear of Yahweh." This reverential awe, this submission to God's ultimate authority and grand majesty, is the foundation upon which all wisdom *must* be built (see, e.g., Job 28:28; Ps. 111:10; Prov. 1:7; Eccles. 12:13). This message and its application was developed by means of reflection on the part of the writers as they were inspired by the Spirit of God.

---

[6]In fact, Proverbs 22:17–24:22 is closely related to the earlier Egyptian wisdom of Amen-em-ope(t). The most recent study is by John Ruffle, "The Teaching of Amenemope and Its Connection with the Book of Proverbs," *Tyndale Bulletin,* vol. 28 (1977), pp. 29–68.

THE PROBLEM WITH GENERALIZATIONS

Now any scheme such as this is open to severe criticism if it is pressed too far. It would be a mistake to look upon this approach as anything more than a very broad generalization. For we have revelation in all three sections of the Old Testament literature discussed thus far. There are passages of direct revelation in the prophets, the Psalms, and the wisdom texts.[7] Further, there are Psalms within the prophetic books and hymns within wisdom texts.[8] Finally, there are wisdom materials in both the Psalms and the prophets.[9]

Although a simplification, the above plan may have merit in showing some of the distinctions in the literatures of the Old Testament Scriptures. All of the Scriptures are inspired, but not all of the Scriptures have the same revelational emphasis. Some of the texts of the Old Testament have the language of response, and other passages display the language of reflection.

EMOTION IN THE PSALMS

This concept helps us to understand the strong emotions in some of the Psalms, particularly as found in the laments. Hear some of these shouts of accusation to God:

Will you forget me forever? (Ps. 13:1)
Why do You hide Yourself in times of trouble? (Ps. 10:1b)

---

[7]Psalm 110 can only be understood as the result of direct revelation. Further, it is difficult to imagine the message of Proverbs 8 apart from direct revelation.

[8]Isaiah 12 is a hymn of praise that could easily fit into the Psalter. Some sections of Job fluctuate between hymnic and wisdom expression.

[9]Several of the Psalms are wisdom poems. Among these are Psalms 1, 8, 19, 111, 119, 139. Wisdom themes are found in selected texts in Isaiah and Jeremiah by some writers. Some believe that Genesis 1 may have a wisdom cast to it; so master's thesis by R. Dennis Cole, Western Baptist Seminary, 1978.

Why have You forsaken me? (Ps. 22:1)
My Rock, do not be deaf to me! (Ps. 28:1)

We would be greatly mistaken if we regarded these statements as *revelation* in the strictest sense of that term. For in these Psalms the initial complaint is proven to be wrong. As a matter of fact:

God does not forget His people (see e.g., Is. 49:15,16).
God does not hide Himself in troubled times (see e.g., Ps. 139:7–12).
God does not forsake His servant (see e.g., Is. 54:10).
God is never deaf to His own (see e.g., Ex. 2:24).

Nevertheless, these complaints are *inspired* by God, for in the language of response they truly reflect the troubles of God's people living in a difficult world. These are expressions of how they—and we!—sometimes feel. These are real to them, and they may be real to us as well. God *uses* these expressions of doubt and despair to magnify His name as He leads the troubled believer to a new sense of confidence in His matchless character.

THE PENTATEUCH OF PRAISE

I trust that during the course of reading these chapters you have been paging through the Book of Psalms as well, reading here and reveling there. I hope that you have become more intimately related to this textbook on praise. It may be that in your musings you have observed that the Psalter is composed of *five books*. This pentateuchal arrangement calls to mind the Pentateuch of Moses, the Torah. The five books of the Psalms are as follows:

Book I	Psalms 1–41
Book II	Psalms 42–72
Book III	Psalms 73–89

Book IV   Psalms 90–106
Book V   Psalms 107–150

The reason for the fivefold division of the Book of Psalms is not known. Some writers on the Psalms believe that they have found a thematic arrangement wherein the Psalms of the first book relate to the theme of the Book of Genesis, the Psalms of the second book relate to the message of Exodus, and so on through the five books of each pentateuch.

My personal feeling is that such a practice is very difficult to demonstrate. It is hard to show how Psalm 114, for example, which is a Psalm of the Exodus would be in Book Five, which should correspond, according to the theory, to the Book of Deuteronomy. Again, why is Psalm 104, which speaks so fully of creation, in Book Four, which is to correspond to the Book of Numbers? Many such problems with this theory may be given.

It would appear that the arrangement into five books was not designed to be thematically correspondent to the Pentateuch of Moses, but rather, as Christoph Barth suggests, was a more general "five-fold answer of the congregation to the word of God—in the five books of Moses."[10] This concept of a "five-fold answer to God's Word" fits nicely with the approach stressed earlier in this chapter, that the Psalms are the language of response to the prophetic word. I believe then that we ought not try to find any but the most general sense of comparison between the two pentateuchs.[11]

A COLLECTION OF CODAS

Each of the books of the Psalms ends with a doxology. *Book One,* Psalms 1–41, ends with the doxology of Psalm 41:13:

[10]Barth, *Introduction,* p. 4.
[11]We may mention that the critical approach to the Bible has turned things a bit upside down. The older critics condensed the composition of the Psalms to a generation or so late in the history of Israel, and expanded the writings of Moses to a millennium.

> Blessed be Yahweh, the God of Israel,
> From everlasting to everlasting.
> Amen and Amen.

Book Two, Psalms 42–72, concludes with the doxology of Psalm 72:18,19:

(18) Blessed be Yahweh God, the God of Israel,
      Who alone works wonders.
(19) And blessed be His glorious name forever;
      And may the whole earth be filled with His glory.
      Amen and Amen.

To this doxology is appended the editorial note of an early age, Psalm 72:20,

> The prayers of David the son of Jesse are ended.[12]

Book Three, Psalms 73–89, has this doxology in Psalm 89:52,

> Blessed be Yahweh forever!
> Amen and Amen.

Book Four, Psalms 90–106, gives this doxology in Psalm 106:48,

> Blessed be Yahweh, the God of Israel,
> From everlasting even to everlasting.
> And let all the people say, "Amen."
> Hallelujah!

Book Five, Psalms 107–150, ends with a doxology that is the entire 150th Psalm:

---

[12]On the possible meaning of this note, see below, p. 103.

(1) Hallelujah!
Praise God in His sanctuary;
Praise Him in His mighty expanse,
(2) Praise Him for His mighty deeds;
Praise Him according to His excellent greatness.

(3) Praise Him with trumpet sound;
Praise Him with harp and lyre.
(4) Praise Him with timbrel and dancing;
Praise Him with stringed instruments and pipe.
(5) Praise Him with loud cymbals;
Praise Him with resounding cymbals.

(6) Let everything that has breath praise Yahweh!
Hallelujah!

As we have seen throughout, praise is a matter of life and breath. This Psalm so asserts! Moreover, it seems certain that this Psalm was written especially to conclude the whole book, just as Psalm 1 seems to have been composed particularly to introduce the collection.

These words of Psalm 150 are words of incredible power and emotion. Sometimes we just leave these words "on the page." Peter E. Gillquist describes a worship service in which this Psalm was acted out in the church. The congregational procession was followed by instrumental music, dancing, clapping, and vocal praise to God as the Psalm indicates. In this physical enactment of the Psalm, these old words took on new life that animated the people greatly. Gillquist states, "My heart was filled with such thanksgiving and praise that tears began to come to my eyes as I realized I was seeing a foretaste of what worship in heaven will be like."[13] We dare not leave these words on the page.

[13]Peter E. Gillquist, *The Physical Side of Being Spiritual* (Grand Rapids: Zondervan, 1979), p. 125.

FROM STREAMS TO RIVER

At this point I wish to attempt to simplify a difficult issue, the manner of the composition and collection of the Psalms. Over the period of one thousand years, that is, from the time of Moses when Israel was a youth, until the time of her maturity under the restoration of Ezra, believer-poets were writing praise hymns and lament songs as they responded to the words of God in a hostile world. These poems were composed by men and women, by kings and by commoners.

Some of the Psalms were written by David who knelt beside his grazing sheep in recognition that he was like a lamb of the Great Shepherd. Other hymns were written by professional guild musicians specifically for temple worship. Still other poems were composed by wise men in the instruction of their charges. Yet other compositions were set to poetry at the express direction of the oracle of the Spirit; for, as was suggested earlier, some of the Psalms are indeed prophetic and revelational in the strictest sense.

However these varied Psalms were written, ultimately many were collected into groups for the good of the community in its worship to the living God. We do not have to suppose that every Psalm was expressly composed for the community. Many were likely intended by their composers to remain private and personal. Some of the Psalms in the Bible were not put into the collection of the Psalter, but rather were added to the prophetic or prose texts of various books of the Bible at places where they would most naturally enhance the narrative. So we have the Psalm of Hannah in 1 Samuel 2 and the song of Deborah in Judges 5. There are Psalms in the prophetic books as well. The millennial Psalm of Isaiah (Is. 12) climaxes the first section of that book (chapters 1–12). The Psalm of Daniel 2 and that of Jonah 2 are other examples. Further, we have an example of a Psalm of David that is in the historical narrative (2 Sam. 22) as well as being in the Psalter (Ps. 18). A large number of the Psalms of ancient

Israel were collected through the ages, however, to comprise the Book of Psalms as we have it today.

The analogy for the collection of the Book of Psalms that is most helpful is that which is suggested by Barth in his *Introduction*. He compares the process to the growth of a river:

> Anyone who seeks to understand this development should think of the way a *river* is formed: it takes innumerable little springs and streams to feed even the brook, and many brooks and small rivers must flow into its long meandering course before the full width of the river flows down to the sea![14]

As the Mississippi River begins rather unpretentiously in northern Minnesota, but then becomes the "Father of Waters," Old Man River, some twenty-five hundred miles later as it flows into the Gulf of Mexico, so the Psalms began as individual units and small collections that merged into larger and larger collections until the whole was complete.

COLLECTORS AND COLLECTIONS

Some of the early collecting activity may be attributed to David, the sweet singer of Israel. Seventy-three Psalms in the Old Testament collection are attributed to him, and two other songs are said to be his by writers of the New Testament.[15] It is highly possible that he was responsible for most of Book I in its present form, with the exception of Psalm 1, which is likely a later composition.

The second book of Psalms contains largely Davidic mate-

[14]Barth, *Introduction,* pp. 2–3.

[15]David is credited in the superscriptions as author of Psalms 3–9, 11–32, 34–41, 51–65, 68–70, 86, 101, 103, 108–110, 122, 124, 131, 133, 138–145. New Testament writers credit him with Psalms 2 (Acts 4:25) and Solomon wrote two Psalms (72,127). One each is credited to Moses (90), Ethan (89), and Heman (88). Psalms 1,10,33,43,66,67,71,91–94,96–100,102,104–107, 111–121,123,125,126,128–130,132,134–137,146–150 are anonymous.

rials, but the last Psalm in this cluster was written by Solomon. It may be that Solomon was responsible for this collection, to which he added his own composition. He termed the collection, "The Prayers of David the Son of Jesse" (as we read in Ps. 72:20).

It would be guesswork to state with any precision who would have been responsible for the collecting and editing of the three subsequent books. We should say, however, that the presence of Davidic Psalms within these later collections is entirely possible on the basis of independent Psalms not included within earlier books.

Mini-collections seem to have existed for special functions. One notable such mini-hymnal is the collection of "Psalms of Ascents" (Pss. 120–134). These Psalms were assembled for worship reasons from earlier materials, much like the five books used in the annual feasts of Israel (Ruth, Lamentations, Ecclesiastes, Song of Solomon, and Esther) were put in a special collection in the Writings (the *Kethubim,* the third division of the Hebrew canon). The pilgrims who made their treks to Jerusalem to worship in the temple were given small hymnals to guide and direct them in their spiritual pilgrimage "up" to Jerusalem. Yet another mini-collection is the Hallel Hymnal (Pss. 104–106;111–117;135; and perhaps 146–150). Many of these Psalms are still read by Jewish people on the Passover *Seder.* A third small collection is the group of Royal Psalms (Pss. 93–99).

We know that some of the Psalms have been divided into smaller sections for the purpose of worship in Israel. For example, by the refrains in Psalm 42:5,11 and 43:5, we believe that these two Psalms were originally one poem. The refrain is,

> Why are you in despair, O my soul?
> And why have you become disturbed within me?
> Hope in God, for I shall again praise Him,
> For the help of His presence (42:5 NASB).

Again, many scholars believe that Psalms 9 and 10 were originally one composition because of the remnants of an acrostic pattern that goes from the first letter of the Hebrew alphabet (*aleph*) to the eleventh letter (*kaph*) in Psalm 9. Psalm 10 carries us through the twenty-second letter. However, the full acrostic nature of Psalms 9 and 10 is not presently observable.[16]

Another indication of editorial work for worship patterns may include Psalm 117. Its brevity (two verses) may be accounted for as the result of a section of a longer Psalm being separated for the purposes of the worshiping community. This Psalm may have been used in the liturgy of Israel as a call for praise in the worship service. This suggests a pattern that good community worship should combine structure and spontaneity. Today we seem to find this balance difficult.

RESHAPING IN THE PSALMS

The Psalms show reshaping and reworking as well. Psalm 14 is essentially the same poem as Psalm 53. They are distinguished in the last verses of each Psalm, and in the use of *Yahweh* in Psalm 14 where Psalm 53 has *Elohim* (God). The relative distribution of the words *Yahweh* and *Elohim* in Books One and Two has led to the convention of calling Book One *Yahwistic* and Book Two *Elohistic*.

The Psalms also quote from one another. Psalm 108, which is in Book Five, is actually the combination of two sections from two other Psalms. That is, Psalm 108:1–5 is taken from Psalm 57:7–11. The balance of Psalm 108 (vv. 6–13) is taken from Psalm 60:5–12. Both of the earlier Psalms that Psalm 108 quotes were written by David. The superscription "of David" in Psalm 108 is correct, though the "patching" may

[16]Acrostic Psalms include 9–10, 25, 34, 111, 112, 119, 145. Acrostic patterns are found elsewhere in the Old Testament, e.g., Lam. 3, Nah. 1:1–10 (incomplete).

have been done by later editors. One may think of a Broadway musical from which a medley of songs might be arranged. When that medley is announced, credit for the composition had better be given to the original composer.

THE SPIRIT AND THE PSALMS

All of these indicators within the Book of Psalms suggest that the gathering of these poems was most complex. Over all and through all, however, we must see the superintending work of the Spirit of God as He directed the employment of these poems for His own purposes in the worship patterns of Israel of old as well as for His purposes in these poems in the community of the faithful today. Though the Psalms are the language of response, they, too, are part of the "all Scripture" that was inspired by God for our good.

NOW HEAR THEM SING!

As we conclude these introductory chapters on the Book of Psalms, I wish to stress again that *praise is a matter of life and breath*. This chapter has had a heavy share of the details of the Psalms that might, if not taken in perspective, cause the Psalms to cease to sing for you. For this reason I feel that the best way to conclude this chapter, and Part One of the book, is to present some selections from the Psalms (all in the NASB version), and simply *let them sing*.

Listen first to Psalm 63:1–5. Let the poetry of praise do its wonderwork in you.

(1) O God, Thou art my God; I shall seek Thee earnestly;
      My soul thirsts for Thee, my flesh yearns for Thee,
      In a dry and weary land where there is no water.

(2)   Thus I have beheld Thee in the sanctuary,
      To see Thy power and Thy glory.

(3)   Because Thy lovingkindness is better than life,
      My lips will praise Thee.

(4)   So I will bless Thee as long as I live;
      I will lift up my hands in Thy name.

(5)   My soul is satisfied as with marrow and fatness.
      And my mouth offers praises with joyful lips.

Did you read this aloud? Did you observe the vocabulary of praise? Did the Psalm do its work in you? Are you ready to act out the praise this Psalm presents?

Here is another selection of praise from the hymnal of Israel. This is Psalm 104:31–35. The translation again is the NASB, but *Yahweh* has been substituted for LORD and *Hallelujah* for *Praise the LORD*.

(31)   Let the glory of Yahweh endure forever;
      Let Yahweh be glad in His works:

(32)   He looks at the earth, and it trembles;
      He touches the mountains, and they smoke.

(33)   I will sing to Yahweh as long as I live;
      I will sing praise to my God while I have my being.

(34)   Let my meditation be pleasing to Him;
      As for me, I shall be glad in Yahweh.

(35)   Let sinners be consumed from the earth,
      And let the wicked be no more.
        Bless Yahweh, O my soul.
        Hallelujah!

Read again the words of verse 33. Praise is what life is about! The Psalms of Israel do not speak of a life of faith where there is no praise to God.

Psalm 104:33 leads me to think of Psalm 146:2. Both verses assert the thesis of our book concerning praise and life itself.

Here is the great hymn of praise, Psalm 146, in its entirety, again from the NASB with my substitutions. Read this prayerfully, and see how much is taught and enjoyed concerning the God of all praise.

(1) Hallelujah!
    Praise Yahweh, O my soul!
(2) I will praise Yahweh while I live;
    I will sing praises to my God while I have my being.
(3) Do not trust in princes,
    In mortal man, in whom there is no salvation.
(4) His spirit departs, he returns to the earth;
    In that very day his thoughts perish.
(5) How blessed is he whose help is the God of Jacob,
    Whose hope is in Yahweh his God;
(6) Who made heaven and earth,
    The sea and all that is in them;
    Who keeps faith forever;
(7) Who executes justice for the oppressed;
    Who gives food to the hungry.
    Yahweh sets the prisoners free.
(8) Yahweh opens the eyes of the blind;
    Yahweh raises up those who are bowed down;
    Yahweh loves the righteous;
(9) Yahweh protects the strangers;
    He supports the fatherless and the widow;
    But He thwarts the way of the wicked.
(10) Yahweh will reign forever,
    Thy God, O Zion, to all generations.
                        HALLELUJAH!

All we who have life and breath join in these ancient words to give praise to Your name our great God!

Hallelujah! Praise Yahweh!

PART TWO

Enjoying the Psalms

CHAPTER 8

Psalm 113
Hallelujah!
The Will of God for You

In everything give thanks;
for this is the will of God
in Christ Jesus for you.
—1 Thessalonians 5:18 NKJB

One of my sources of enjoyment is what I call "recreational reading." This is a diversion from the tube and a good source of relaxation from the more demanding reading I am involved in during the day. While I try to keep some variety in my reading, I am a small-time "buff" on a minor genre, mystery fiction. I can get engrossed fairly quickly in an old-fashioned "whodunit" by Dorothy L. Sayers, Agatha Christie, or P. D. James.

A few years ago I came across a writer of detective fiction, Dell Shannon, who has as one of her protagonists a homicide detective who is an evangelical Christian. Detective Piggot is as regular in his attendance at church as his busy schedule will allow. He attends Wednesday evening services and choir practice. He has his eye on a soprano in the choir but moves very slowly. It took several books for him to ask her out for coffee after choir practice.

My "find" is orthodox in his reverence toward Christ, his reliance on the integrity of the Scriptures, and his realization of the machinations of Satan in an evil world. Yet, one thing bothers me about my Christian detective. *He does not sound the praise of God.* Not once in several books have I read a passage where he exults in the wonder of Yahweh.

Now one may say, "How can you expect a policeman on the homicide bureau of the Los Angeles Police Department to praise God?" In the foul sewer of humanity in which he swims, what would *he* encounter that would encourage praise to God? Yet (brace yourself!) such an attitude is merely a "cop-out." Praise is due God irrespective of our circumstances or setting in life. We may not wish to praise Him for our trouble, but we may always praise Him for who He is and for what He does.

The Christian life was meant to be a full chord. Often the missing note in our harmonies is the note of praise. One of the most important issues presented in the Psalms is that praise is due God by the believer. Praise is not an option nor an elective. It is an obligation.

In our short stay in the Philippines my family and I learned an expression that speaks of a binding obligation of gratitude. This is the Tagalog phrase, *utang na loob*. When applied to some interpersonal relationships, such an obligation can be debilitating, as one never escapes the feeling of obligation to a benefactor. But this is the very concept we must have in mind in terms of our relationship to our Redeemer God! We *are* under an enduring obligation of gratitude to Him—and this is a happy state.

Psalm 113 states this truth most clearly: *Praise is due His incomparable name.* The importance of praise and its rationale in the mind of God are displayed vividly in this Psalm.

THE IMPERATIVE OF PRAISE

Psalm 113 is an anonymous Psalm of Descriptive Praise. It has nine verses and is made of three movements of three verses each. The first movement, or strophe, may be read as follows.

(1) Praise Yah!
Praise, O servants of Yahweh!

Praise the Name Yahweh!
(2) Let the Name Yahweh be blessed,
From this time forth and forever!
(3) From the rising of the sun to its setting,
The Name Yahweh is to be praised!

In this first movement we are confronted at once with the message of the Psalm: *Praise is due the incomparable name of God.* From the opening "Hallelujah" in verse 1 ("Praise Yah"), to the concluding "Hallelujah" at the end of verse 9, this poem overflows with the praise of God. The first movement presents an *imperative* to praise His incomparable name. The imperative is seen in the form of the verbs employed in these verses. All of them are commands.

The Psalm opens with a Hebrew word familiar to Christians all over the world. This is true regardless of their national language or local dialect. This word has followed the expansion of the church universal. This word is "Hallelujah." It is often used but rarely explained.

The word "Hallelujah" is a Hebrew word that is a compound term. It is made of a plural imperative of the verb "to praise" coupled to the short form of the name of God, "Yah" (or "Jah").

But the fact that this word is a command must be stressed. My friend Dr. Ralph Alexander makes the following comparison. If a person were to shout to a crowd of people "Shut the door!" several times, but no one would in fact go and close the door, the command could hardly be said to have been accomplished. Similarly, merely to say, "Praise the Lord" ("Hallelujah")—and not in fact to offer a *response* of praise— is to fall short of the intention of the command.

Praise Is Due His Name

To appreciate the significance of this basic issue in the Psalms, we may approach the first movement as a news reporter might. A first question might be, "*What* is praise?" The number of times words for praise occur in the first three verses demands we ask this question.

113

The key term for praise in this Psalm is the Hebrew verb *hālal*. As noted earlier praise is to be both public and vocal. Each of the words for praise in the Psalms has its own nuance or flavor, however. The word *hālal* has about it the idea of *excited boasting*.

This word is what you say when your ten-year-old boy has just scored in junior soccer. *Hālal* comes when a desired promotion is achieved, when a healthy baby is born, when one gets into a new car for the first time, when the house sale closes, or when you have found a lost contact lens.

This, then, is a very special word for *excited boasting*. If I were to begin to boast about myself, you would quickly term me an egotist. If I were to boast about my children, you would soon term me a bore. (I would not understand that, however.) But if one begins to boast excitedly about God, no one can fault him. He can never exhaust God's splendors nor recall all of His perfections. The Hebrew word translated *praise* in our Psalm is a word used best not of soccer or cars, not of recitals or sales, but of the *living Yahweh*. He is the One who truly deserves our boastful, excited praise.

The High Calling of Slavery

From the *what* of praise, we may now turn to the *who*. That is, *who* is to praise? This Psalm states that the command to praise is addressed to Yahweh's *servants* (v. 1b). The title is hardly one many of today's young people would give on a form asking for career expectations.

During our stay in Manila we enjoyed and appreciated the tremendous help of a house-girl. We found her help to be a necessity. Terminology was difficult, however. Our children called her *Ate* ("big sister") Lourdes. My wife and I settled on "our helper," when describing her to others. The words "maid" or "servant" seem to be demeaning. But even less lofty is the word in our Psalm. Basically it means *slave*. Yet it is to God's slaves that this command to praise His name is given.

In the Old Testament world where slavery was a fact of life, there was, we believe, a relative status even among slaves. Not only were there slaves over other slaves within a given household, there was also a relative status among slaves depending upon the wealth and position of the owner. If one slave were owned by a master of ten, and another by an owner of thirty, the slave of the grander master had some little something over the slave of the poorer household. Joseph's position as a slave in Egypt had double honor. Not only was he over all the other slaves of the household (see Gen. 39:5,6); his master was an officer of Pharaoh (see Gen. 39:1).

The poets of the Bible applied this cultural logic to one's relationship to God. If one were regarded as His slave, there could be no greater position. *For there is no grander master than He.* Hence, to be a slave of the living Yahweh is the highest title to which believers can aspire. Kings would do well to hope to be His slaves!

Israel as a nation was called to be the slave people of Yahweh. Yet she failed repeatedly in her servitude. Some men and women of Israel were faithful servants, however, obeying the commands of their Master gladly. The Servant of servants, the slave of God *par excellence,* is the Lord Jesus Christ. By prophetic oracle (see Is. 52:13–53:12) and living fulfillmcnt (see Phil. 2:5–8), He embodied and fleshed-out the servant ideal. It is likely for this reason that Paul delighted to call himself a bondslave of Jesus Christ (see Rom. 1:1).

Our relationship to God through the Lord Jesus Christ is immeasurably better than that which Israel had under the Sinaitic Covenant. Jesus called His followers "friends" rather than "slaves" (John 15:15). Further, Paul says we are "sons" where we were formerly "slaves" (Gal. 4:7). Nevertheless, there is an important sense in which servanthood is still a New Testament ideal. This is true because it depicts our readiness to obey and magnify our great God. If anything describes a servant rightly, it is his or her readiness to obey the command of the master. The command we have here from our Master in this Psalm is to give praise to His great name.

115

We Praise His Name

To whom is praise to be given? To ask this question is to answer it. For Psalm 113 emphasizes most forcefully the direction of praise. In the first three verses, the name of God is given no less than *five times* as the object of praise. The phrase, "the name of the LORD" (better, "the name Yahweh"), is crucial to an understanding of Old Testament theology.

By this phrase the poets of the Bible employ a symbol or cipher summarizing all that God is. In the name of God we are confronted with a capsule form of all of His excellences. A beloved Old Testament scholar of an earlier generation, H. C. Alleman, wrote: "The name is His renown, the disclosure of Himself in the world."[1]

To praise the name of God is to say with integrity something right about God. When we say that "God is good," we are praising His name. Similarly, the following are a few examples of genuine statements of praise about the living Yahweh:

> The Lord is great!
> His majesty is resplendent!
> He has been so good to me!
> God never changes!
> Jesus is my Savior!

Usually the Old Testament terms for praise include the nuance of excitement or intensity. Praise is not done casually or superficially. But as one responds to the reality of the living God as revealed in the Scriptures, *words of praise* are demanded to exalt His name. These words may be spoken or sung. But they must come if His name is to be praised.

[1]H.C. Alleman, "Devotional Studies Based on Psalms," in J.M. Myers, O. Reimherr, and H.N. Bream, *Biblical Studies in Memory of H. C. Alleman* (Locust Valley, N.Y.: J.J. Augustin, 1960), p. 46.

But When And Where?

One might then ask, "*When* is praise to be given to the name of God?" The Psalm is quite clear on the time factor. Verse 2b reads, "From this time forth and forever." It may be that this command to praise the name of God was articulated to you a long time ago. In that case, the command is already operative in your life. If, however, in reading this chapter you are being confronted with this command for the first time, then you should note today's date and write it here: _____ . Go ahead, write this down, for *from this time forth* praise is due His name from you.

And how long shall this praise be due? In the words of the popular hymn "Amazing Grace,"

When we've been there ten thousand years,
Bright, shining as the sun,
We've no less days to sing God's praise,
Than when we first begun.

From this time forth and forever, praise is due His incomparable name.

A last question is *where?* Where is one to praise God? The psalmist answers: Wherever you happen to be. In verse 3 he uses a poetic image of the sun rising and setting to depict the directions east and west. Wherever the sun does its duty, you and I are to do ours. Our task—our happy obligation—is to give praise to our Lord.

Some have thought that the words "from the rising of the sun to its setting" mean "from dawn to dusk." Once, when I was to preach from this passage, another person gave my message the unhappy title, "From Sunrise to Sunset." This type of interpretation would logically exclude praise at night! The time factor is given in verse 2. Verse 3 speaks of geography. To repeat, praise is due His incomparable name wherever we happen to be.

This first movement gives the reader an imperative to praise the incomparable name Yahweh. Praise is excited boasting. It is to be done by those who are His servants. Praise is to be directed to His great name, which is the symbol of all that He is. Praise is to be given from now on, wherever we happen to be. The imperative is clear; the task of obedience is a happy chore. *There is an imperative to praise His incomparable name.*

THE EXPLANATION: INCOMPARABILITY

In the second movement of Psalm 113, verses 4–6, the writer of our poem does something extraordinary. *He explains* the imperative of praise. Commanders don't normally explain their commands. In the military there are many clichés about obedience, such as, "When told to jump, ask how high on the way up." Echoing the words of Kipling, soldiers are to say, "Ours is not to reason why, ours is but to do or die." These concepts of implicit obedience are deemed necessary to develop disciplined battle readiness in army troops. I am told that the Jesuit priests have a similar saying (in Latin) which means "[obedience] as a corpse!"

I find it most remarkable that in the context of the present Psalm, the command to praise the name of God is explained by God. It seems that God is willing, even desirous, to do that which human officers are most often unwilling or unable to do. He answers the question, "Why?" Although He is the commanding General of the universe, God shows us that His order is reasonable. This seems to be another example of His condescending grace. These are the words:

(4) High above all nations is Yahweh,
    Surpassing the heavens is His glory!
(5) Who is like Yahweh our God,
    Who exalts Himself in sitting,

118

(6) Who humbles Himself to see,
   Things in heaven and in the earth?

The explanation of the imperative to praise God lies in a central factor of His excellence: *He is incomparable.* The incomparability of Yahweh has been an almost forgotten emphasis of Old Testament theology. Although stressed repeatedly by the poets and prophets of the Bible, God's incomparability has been given such scant attention by scholars that it was not until recently that the first major treatise was written on this great subject.[2]

Despite our inattention to it, this joyous fact is paramount in the Psalms. There is no one like God. There is nothing that may be compared to Him. The psalmist who wrote our poem stresses Yahweh's incomparability in three spheres: (1) He is incomparable in His position, (2) He is incomparable in His person, and (3) He is incomparable in His passion.

High Above All

It might be easy to "ho-hum" our way through the first part of verse 4, "Yahweh is high above all nations." The words really are significant, however. This Psalm was written in the cultural context of a polytheistic world. "Gods" vied with each other for superiority in the imagination of men. Further, the "power" of many deities was believed to be geographically conditioned. A god of one nation would not be effective in another city. But Yahweh, the God of reality, is God over all nations. He is not conditioned by geography in any way whatsoever. Yahweh *is* high above all nations!

As our own country was traumatized by our national nightmare of surprise, betrayal, and deceit in the Watergate years, it has become increasingly more important, even in

---

[2]This is the study by C.J. Labuschagne, *The Incomparability of Yahweh in the Old Testament,* Pretoria Oriental Series, ed. A. Van Selms (Leiden, The Netherlands: E. J. Brill, 1966). Both author and editor insist that this is the first serious study on this subject in the history of the church.

our own culture, to remember that there are no surprises for God. Above all nations and their leaders, the Lord is high, exalted, and ultimately in control. He is over the United States and Canada, over the Soviet Union and China, over Papua New Guinea and Mozambique, over Israel, Syria, and Iran. No nation, no national leadership, no local deity may be compared to Him.

It is the second member of verse 4 that staggers our imagination and explodes our petty views. Not only is Yahweh above all nations, but His glory transcends the universe. By definition this must be true. The Creator may not be overshadowed in His own creation. Our universe, we are told by current theory, is a finite creation that is expanding at an incredible rate. But beyond the hundreds of billions of stars that God has sprinkled throughout His vast universe is His own limitless glory—uncontained, unrivaled, unmeasured, unknowable except by His own mind!

Nothing may be compared to Him! No one may be set beside Him. Why, the oceans He measures in the palm of His hand, and the vastness of the heavens He describes by His span (the distance from the out-stretched thumb to the little finger; see Is. 40:12). In His position He is beyond all description.

Who Is Like Our God?

Psalm 113:5a asks, "Who is like Yahweh our God?" This is not the question of a petty religious chauvinist challenging a Moabite or an Edomite with the childish ploy, "My God is better than your god!" Rather, here we have the sound assessment of reasoned theology: To whom can you compare the God of reality? To a rock? To a tree? To an ideal? To a job? To a goal? To an unknown power? To the chic, but impersonal and divided "Force" of *Star Wars?* To anything good or evil in all the universe?

No! To nothing may He be compared. To no one may He be likened. All their gods are "compounded zeroes" as Psalm

96:5 declares. But He, and He alone, is the eternal, personal Deity with whom we have to do.

In Isaiah 44:6–8 we have a majestic complement to the words of Psalm 113. These verses sing:

Thus says Yahweh, King of Israel,
Even his Redeemer, Yahweh of Hosts:
"I am the first and I am the last,
And over and apart from Me there is no God.
For who is like Me? Let him proclaim it!
And let him declare it and arrange his case before Me;
From the time when I established the ancient nation;
And coming things, even those which are yet to be, let them declare to them.
Stop trembling! Cease to be paralyzed with fright!
Have I not caused you to hear and declared long ago—
And you are My witnesses!—
Is there any God over and apart from Me?
Or any other Rock?
I know of none!"

God in all of His wisdom and knowledge knows of none to be compared to Himself. He is utterly incomparable in His resplendent glory.

The second colon of Psalm 113:5 is regularly rendered, "who is enthroned on high." This is fitting and true, but the translation suggests a passivity to the glory of God that is unknown among the poets and prophets of the Old Testament. Not so elegant, perhaps, but more literal would be this translation: "who exalts Himself in sitting!" That is, even in the act of sitting enthroned, Yahweh is active and dynamic; never is He passive.

Consider Isaiah's vision of the enthroned Yahweh in his palace vision (see Is. 6:1–13). Isaiah saw the Lord high and lifted up, with the trains of His royal robes billowing in the palace throne room. Seraphs were stationed above and all around Him, chanting in antiphonal chorus:

Holy, holy, holy is Yahweh of hosts;
The fullness of the whole earth is His glory! (Is. 6:3).

The very level of their praise caused the foundations of the building to quiver, while the throne room was being filled with smoke. All is in motion. The decibel level is intense. God's glory is dynamic, never static.

Infinity Plus X Equals?

The exaltation of the enthroned Yahweh presents an interesting math question in theology. Since God's glory is infinite, how may glory be added to glory? Even new math would stumble on this one! What base would one use in quantifying God's glory? How may the God of heaven "exalt with respect to sitting"? There is one suggestion, and it is staggering and awesome.

The infinite Yahweh is in need of nothing and has existed in perfect splendor for all eternity. Nevertheless, in His creation of mankind, He accepts praise from His people. So glory *is* added to glory. *Our praise* is added to His immeasurable wonder, and He exalts still grander in His enthronement. "Oh, the depth of the riches both of the wisdom and knowledge of God! How unsearchable are His judgments and unfathomable His ways!" (Rom. 11:33 NASB).

Our Stooping God

Not only is Yahweh incomparable in His position and in His person but also in what we may term His *passion*. Verse 6 reads (as the last part of the question "Who is like Yahweh . . ."):

Who humbles Himself to behold
The things that are in heaven and in the earth?

Were we left with verses 4 and 5, we might become Transcendentalists, so impressed with a God who is so far out there that we would doubt any possibility of His care and concern for those of us "down here."

Yet from His incredibly majestic throne He stoops to see the heavens (itself a condescending act). Then He stoops still lower to meet our needs here on planet Earth. This *stooping of majesty* is the gospel, the good news. The verb used in this verse is a picturesque expression of someone leaning over a balcony or out of a window to view something or someone below. This is "heaven coming down." This is His incomparable passion: God breaks into the space-time-light continuum in stooping grace to meet the needs of His people. It is for this reason that the message of the Psalm is finally and fully explained: Praise *is* due His incomparable name.

ILLUSTRATIONS OF HIS INCOMPARABLE GRACE

The Psalm began with an imperative to praise God. Then it moved to an explanation for that imperative based on His incomparable position, person, and passion. Some of the hearers of this Psalm (then and now) must come from the "Missouri" district of southern Judah. For they need one more statement in response to their "Show me!"

Psalm 113 is not content to tell of the reason for the imperative to praise God. It concludes by giving illustrations of His incomparability in "living color," and not without the image of strong odors either, as we shall see. This lovely hymn presents two illustrations of His condescending grace. Both are taken from very familiar elements of the culture of ancient Israel: poverty and joylessness.

The last movement of our passage reads:

(7) He raises from the dust the poor,
From the ashheap He exalts the needy.

(8) To make them sit with princes,
     With the princes of His people.
(9) He makes the barren woman abide in the house
     As a joyful mother of children.
          Praise Yah!

A Wretch on a Heap

The first example that the psalmist uses is that of a man who is desperately poor. The cities of ancient Palestine were quite small because they were confined to the tops of hills or *tels*. In the long processes of continuing reoccupation of a site by successive civilizations, the *tel* would grow progressively smaller. The great task of walling a city was another contributor to its small size.

Generally, then, the cities were very congested. The "high rent" district was within the city walls, for there one might find refuge from enemy armies. The very poor had no place within the city. Rather they lived outside the walls and perhaps existed off other people's garbage, which was cast on the refuse heap outside the city. These festering compost piles describe the meanest location for living the imagination can accommodate. Their stench and smoke provide a picture of hell in the New Testament (in the word *Gehenna,* see, e.g., Mark 9,43,45,47).

Here is a poor wretch. He eats other people's garbage. He is dirty, unkempt, and likely diseased. His level of living is beneath the pale. Then Yahweh looks down. From resplendent glory God stoops. Not just to the city does He bend, but clear to the dunghill Yahweh humbles Himself. To this wretch God condescends. "This is not that for which I have created man, the noblest of all My creation," He declares. He cleans him, dresses him, and brings him inside the walls of the city to the dwelling of princes. There He has this formerly poor man seated at the banquet table of the nobles.

When has God ever done that? He has done it whenever He has lifted a sinner from the festering stench of his death of sin—and then cleansed him, dressed him in spotless garments by the imputation of the righteousness of Christ, and brought him into the dwelling of princes and caused him to sit with the saints at the table of the King. He did this to *us* when He "blessed us with every spiritual blessing in the heavenly places in Christ" (Eph. 1:3 NASB). The picture of verses 7 and 8 is wonderfully descriptive of justification, the declaring righteous action of our God in Christ (see Rom. 4:24–5:2). Here is our great reason and delight for praising our God.

A Woman in Despair

A second illustration of the incomparability of God, which provides a great reason and delight for praising His name, concerns a woman who is utterly without joy. The culture of ancient Israel provided a ready-made term for joylessness— "barren." If a woman had been married for a number of years and had borne no children, the people believed that such a woman was a defective person. (We should understand that this was the popular belief of the people in the ancient Near East and not the teaching of the Bible.)

Picture a small village of a few hundred people. It is early evening. Groups of women are going to and from the village well. They come in clusters, happily talking about Joshua's new tooth, Rebekah's baby lamb, Simeon's growth spurt, Ari's work in the field—the kinds of things that mothers like to talk about. Then another door opens. The five women already at the well quickly hoist their water jars and hurry home. A cluster of three women decide to stop at Leah's home before proceeding to the well.

The woman who had opened her door walks alone. She is a Hannah. She has been married twelve years, but she has brought reproach to her husband as well as to her father's home. She has no children. Barren! That cold word divided her from all other "normal" women.

Some thought her "ailment" might be catching. She goes to the well alone. Then she returns alone to her husband. Unless he was a most godly man, like the husband of the Hannah of 1 Samuel 1 (Elkanah), he might greet her with the biting words, "I thought I married a woman!" Barren. Joyless.

And then Yahweh looks down. From indescribably exalted glory God stoops. Clear into her misery the incomparable Yahweh humbles Himself. To this barren woman, God in majesty bends in happy condescension. "It was not for joylessness that I made her, the noble partner of man," He declares. He gives to her the only thing that will help her in her culture and life: conception, children. The text states:

He makes the barren woman abide in the house
As a joyful mother of children! (NASB)

Look at that! Diapers are now all over her once immaculate, but empty, house. Children now fill her once lonely hours and her longing arms. She who was barren is now filled with *joy*. And so it is with us. Where we are impoverished, He gives riches. Where we are joyless, He gives great joy.

Again, this is something God has *done*! Another of the great Psalms in the Old Testament was written by just such a woman as is pictured in our Psalm. This was the true Hannah. She was a barren and joyless woman to whom God stooped in majesty and granted conception in response to her great faith. Her Psalm (1 Sam. 2:1–10) forms a moving companion piece to Psalm 113. Hannah gives the original hymnic setting of God's stooping grace to those on the dunghill (see 1 Sam. 2:8).

Further, in a new and wonderfully unexpected way, one of the finest Psalms of the New Testament was also composed by a woman in direct continuity with 1 Samuel 2:1–10 and Psalm 113. This is the "Magnificat" of Mary, the mother of our Lord (see Luke 1:46–55).

In the case of Mary we do not confront a long-married woman who lacks joy because she has no children. Rather, she is a young woman, just engaged, to whom a child might be a great source of embarrassment. Yet, as Yahweh stoops to the need of Hannah in 1 Samuel, and to the woman of the illustration of Psalm 113, so in a new, grander, and even more mysterious way, His majesty bends to Mary. His incomparable grace overshadows her, so that her conception of a child is unique in all of the human family. Mary is the virgin who is bearing the gestating form of the Son of God. She is bearing the Child that is the focus of maternal affection from creation onward. She senses the same sort of wonder as did Hannah—but intensified beyond our imagination because of Yahweh's choice in her.

Thus her great Psalm of praise. And in it are the same elements we have seen in the music of Hannah and Psalm 113. She also speaks of God's incomparability (v. 49b). She also sings of God's satiating the desire of the hungry (v. 53a). She also speaks of God's stooping grace to the humble (v. 52b). And she rejoices particularly in His bestowing miraculous conception (v. 48). Finally, as prompted by the Spirit, she declares that

> He has given help to Israel His servant,
> In remembrance of His mercy,
> As He spoke to our fathers,
> To Abraham and his offspring forever (vv. 54,55 NASB).

Blessed Mary knew that God was not just honoring her. He was in fact bringing into fulfillment the most important aspect of the Abrahamic Covenant. God, in the Incarnation of Jesus Christ, was providing the means for Israel, Yahweh's servant, to be the agent of blessing for "all the families of the earth" (Gen. 12:3c). It is to these truths that Psalm 113 ultimately leads, as the themes of the Psalm are interwoven into the fabric of Mary's Psalm.

While Psalm 113 points back to the song of Hannah and forward to the song of Mary, first and foremost it leads us to the joyful expression of praise to the name of our incomparable Yahweh. The point of the Psalm is simply this: *Praise is due His incomparable name!* With this message given in an imperative, explained, and then illustrated (in the three movements of the poem), the Psalm then ends as it began with the great command:

Hallelujah! Praise Yahweh!

Our response should be to *do* just that, to give praise to His name.

> Praise Him from whom all blessings flow,
> Praise Him all creatures here below,
> Praise Him above ye heavenly host,
> Praise Father, Son, and Holy Ghost!
> Amen.

CHAPTER 9

Psalm 19
The Wonder of the Word

> I sing the mighty pow'r of God
> That made the mountains rise,
> That spread the flowing seas abroad
> And built the lofty skies.
> I sing the wisdom that ordained
> The sun to rule the day;
> The moon shines full at His command,
> And all the stars obey.
>
> —Isaac Watts

Psalm 19 is one of the most familiar and most loved poems in all the Bible. C. S. Lewis declared it to be one of the greatest poems in world literature.[1] The sweep of this Psalm is stunning. It begins with the stars, then moves to the Scriptures, and finally sweeps to one's inmost soul. From heaven above to the heart within, the panorama of this lyric seems to be without parallel.

But it begins with a song of nature, and so shall we.

A SONG OF NATURE

I know of few things more enjoyable than spending a day with one's family in the forested Cascades, hiking or fishing, enwrapped in the cool, clear mountain air, and enjoying the forest towers and textures. At the end of the day, with the

[1]Lewis, *Reflections,* p. 63.

family back in camp together, the simplest of foods becomes a banquet because of the treasures of the surroundings. Then with the dishes washed and darkness approaching, it is time to start the campfire. What a time to talk, to sing, and to enjoy being part of a family!

A campfire is a source of heat that warms one part of you while the other part freezes. But you find yourself drawn to it, staring at the flames. When all are talked-out, when all the songs have been sung, and all the stories told, everyone seems to watch the fire. Then, almost instinctively, one's eyes follow the sparks as they ascend. Trees surround the fire pit, forming a living and natural cathedral spire that stretches toward the very heavens. The sparks fly up, it seems, to the stars!

Leaning way back, you rediscover the wonder of the stars. Away from the lesser, but so distracting, city lights of neon and mercury vapor, you look again at these many distant lights. Hundreds of billions of these stars are above you. Their distances from us, while measured in part, ultimately are beyond our imagination. *And they speak!* They relate the glory of the Creator. From these stars the words of the great old hymn, "How Great Thou Art!" spring to mind. Then the words of an older and even greater hymn come back again, the words of Psalm 19. For this Psalm begins right where you are, in an experience of the stars' message concerning God's glory. The expression of this experience surpasses lyric poetry in any language.

A SONG OF ONE BOOK

Psalm 19 has occasionally been termed, "the Psalm of two books." Such a designation suggests that this Psalm speaks of the "book of creation" and the "book of Scripture." Yet a closer study of this poem suggests that the emphasis is singular—the Scriptures of God. The Psalm *begins* with the heavens, but ultimately this Psalm is not *about* the heavens. *Psalm 19 is a poem about the Bible.*

The structure of Psalm 19 is like a pyramid. The first movement (v. 1–6) and the third (v. 11–14) are the twin bases that support the central section (v. 7–10). The first section leads into the second, and the third reads out from the second; it is the second section that deals with the wonder of God's Word in such a major way. The message of this Psalm may be stated in this way: *Greater than in all creation is the revelation of God's glory in His Word.*

THE HEAVENS REVEAL GOD'S GLORY

David the shepherd, a professional outdoorsman, must have had a far more intimate knowledge of the stars than many of us moderns who only occasionally rediscover them in our retreats from the glaring, but puny, lights of the city. This is how the Psalm begins:

To the choir master; a Psalm of David.

(1) The heavens are proclaiming the glory of God,
And the sky is manifesting the work of His hands.
(2) Day to day pours forth speech,
And night to night reveals knowledge.
(3)   Without speech and without words,
Without their voice being heard;
(4) Through all the earth their call has gone out,
Their utterances to the end of the world.
In them He has placed a tent for the sun,
(5)   Which is as a bridegroom coming out of his chamber,
Rejoicing as an athlete to run his course.
(6)   From the edge of the heavens is its going forth,
And its circuit is to their other edge,
And there is nothing hidden from its heat.

In these first verses we have a graphic presentation of the truth that *God reveals His glory in His creation.* He has built into His works a demonstration of His might that calls for praise to His name. Verse 1 begins the poem in beautifully balanced synonymous parallelism:

> The heavens are proclaiming the glory of God,
> And the sky is manifesting the work of His hands.

The verbs in this verse are translated in the English progressive tense. They describe ongoing, durative action. The message of the heavens is sounded anew with each twinkling of the stars as the mystery of their light interacts with our atmosphere.[2]

Verse 2 develops further the ongoing nature of the message of the heavens, again using a synonymous pattern:

> Day to day pours forth speech,
> And night to night reveals knowledge.

One day "bubbles forth" speech to the next day, and one night speaks to the next night. As a boiling pot bubbles over, so one day cannot contain its news to itself. In never-ending succes-

---

[2]There is a *visual* impact in the original text that may be shown by putting the English words in the order of the Hebrew:

The heavens	*are proclaiming*	*the glory of God*
a	b	c

And the work of His hands—is manifesting—the sky		
c^1	b^1	a^1

This pattern of inversion of elements (where the *a* element comes first in the first colon and last in the second, and the *c* element is last in the first colon and first in the second) is termed *chiastic,* from the Greek letter *Chi,* which looks something like an *x*. Unfortunately, this is one of the elements of the Hebrew text that does not translate well. Such items led one Hebrew poet, H. Bialik, to chide: "Read the Bible in a translation? I'd as soon kiss my bride through a veil!" Nevertheless, the *basic* element of Hebrew poetry, parallelism, may be enjoyed in all languages into which Hebrew poetry has been translated. Robert Alden has demonstrated chiasm in the larger structure of the poems in his *Psalms,* 3 vols. (Chicago: Moody, 1974–77).

sion the message is relayed, as a baton is passed from one runner to the next. The message is the revelation of the glory of God.

The word translated "God" in verse 1 is a Hebrew term that is likely related to a root meaning *might*. So the Hebrew word "God" may also be translated as "the Mighty One." It is His glory and His might that are displayed in creation. His essential deity is demonstrated in what He has made. This is what Paul referred to in Romans 1:20:

> For since the creation of the world His invisible attributes, His eternal power and divine nature, have been clearly seen, being understood through what has been made, . . . (NASB).

It is precisely His might and deity that the heavens proclaim. In Genesis 1:1 the plural form *Elohim* is used by Moses as a plural of respect or majesty. This intensive plural in Genesis 1:1 connotes "the Most Mighty One." He who has all might is the Creator of all things. In Genesis 1 and in Psalm 19 Moses and David are particularly careful to use those words that demonstrate the particular revelation of God that creation presents.[3]

Nothing is learned from the stars about God's grace or His ethical character. The heavens are mute about His loyal love. Despite the attempts of some allegorists to find in astrology (!) some semblance of the gospel, it is not there displayed. The stars speak. But their message is circumscribed. The heavens make manifest the deity and might of the Creator. This they sing well, but this is the extent of their song.

Not only does the first verse of our Psalm speak of the ongoing revelation of the glory of God's might by the heavens, it

---

[3]Moses does not speak of God as *Yahweh* until Genesis 2 where the Creator is relating Himself to man. Beginning at 2:4 the words LORD-God *(Yahweh-Elohim)* stress the fact that the God of Creation is the God of relationship. So in Psalm 19, David does not use the name of God until verse 7 when he speaks of His Word.

also presents a marvelous perspective of the Creator vis-à-vis that which He has made. In the words "the work of His hands," we sense the poet is suggesting something about the relationship of the Creator to the created thing.

Despite the genuinely staggering immensity of space and the vast number of stars sprinkled throughout it, we are meant to be overwhelmed by God and not by His product! Similarly, the beauty of God's creation is designed to produce in us the worship of the Creator's beauty. This is stated so nicely in the great Lutheran hymn, "Beautiful Saviour."

> Fair are the meadows,
> Fairer still the woodlands,
> Robed in the blooming garb of spring;
> Jesus is fairer,
> Jesus is purer,
> Who makes the woeful heart to sing.

David, in a subtle expression, produces the desired response by suggesting that all the cosmos is merely "the work of His hands" (v. 1b). The universe is God's handicraft! It demonstrates His might and deity, but it is ever less impressive than He. For the Creator can never be contained in that which He has made. Vast, immense, and staggering as the universe truly is, it is merely the fingerwork of an incredibly greater and more magnificent Deity. God's heavens are the work of His fingers.[4]

The expression in this Psalm reminds me of a photograph that appeared in *Life* magazine some years ago. Roosevelt Greer, a huge football player, was shown sitting in a rocking chair doing needlepoint! With all of his latent, brute strength, this former gridiron hero was at work on a dainty handicraft.

[4]In another Psalm, David ponders: "When I consider the heavens, / the work of Your fingers, ..." (Ps. 8:3a). Further, the human fetus is also depicted as Yahweh's exquisite handicraft in Psalm 139:13–16. This is argued in my pamphlet on abortion, *In Celebrating Love of Life,* pp. 6–8.

Perhaps God's relationship to the universe may be similarly pictured. Creation demonstrates His might; but from the vantage point of God's infinite power, the creation of all the universe was finger-play.[5]

BUT NOT IN WORDS

Verse 3 declares that the revelation of the heavens is apart from speech, words, or sound:

> Without speech and without words,
> Without their voice being heard.[6]

Staring at a gnarled and weathered tree, contemplating a delicate, hybrid tea bicolor rose, relaxing beside a running brook, or marveling at the roar of ocean waves are delightful and exhilarative ways of experiencing the revelation of God's might and seeing His deity in His creation. But in a lifetime one cannot sit long enough under that tree to hear words from it. The rose will wilt and go to seed having given no sound. The brook and the waves, with all of their bubble and roar, are incapable of human speech. This is the limitation of God's revelation through His creation.

This revelation is *nonverbal*. Only a fool would deny the power of nonverbal communication. From a lover's gentle

---

[5]Whereas God rested on the seventh day (Gen. 2:2), it was not from fatigue (!), but to demonstrate that He had completed the task. (He never sleeps nor slumbers; see Ps. 121:3b,4.) Creation demonstrates His might; but from the vantage point of God's infinite power, the creation of all the universe was finger-play! Job says: "Look, these are but the fringes of His ways; / What faint whisper we hear of Him! / But who could ever abide His roar?" (Job 26:14). A similar translation is given by M.H. Pope in *The Anchor Bible: Job* (Garden City, N.Y.: Doubleday, 1965).

[6]The KJV translators inserted the word *where,* so that the verse reads: "There is no speech, nor language, / *where* their voice is not heard." Modern translations such as the NASB have dropped this confusing insertion. The KJV translators were always fair to their readers, however. All such insertions were given in *italics.*

caress to the silent stance of a hooded Klansman, from a baby's smile to the clenched fist of a campus radical—all of us have experienced the power of nonverbal communication. Yet because it is apart from words, this type of communication is most subject to misinterpretation.

Natural revelation, though universal, may be misunderstood. This is not to slander creation, but to understand it. We do not indict God's handiwork, but we do insist that it may be abused. It is a nonverbal revelation that has gone out to all the earth (v. 4a,b). All are "without excuse" (Rom. 1:20), for the call[7] and utterances of the heavens have extended to the "edge of the world."

AS A BRIDEGROOM

The great witness by day is the sun. David rhapsodizes:

> (4c) In them He has placed a tent for the sun,
> (5) Which is as a bridegroom coming out of his chamber,
> Rejoicing as an athlete to run his course.
> (6) From the edge of the heavens is its going forth,
> And its circuit is to their other edge,
> And there is nothing hidden from its heat!

This section could only have been written in a part of the world where the sun is a most robust and virile factor in daily living. In the arid climate of southern Judah where David lived, the sun is an ever-present reality. It belongs to that sky as though God Himself had pitched a tent for it.

The figures of "bridegroom" and "athlete" are particularly fitting in that part of the world. No one who has ever walked the Jericho Road in heat of over 110 degrees can doubt that

[7]*Call,* instead of surveyor's *line* (NASB), is defended well by Dahood in *Psalms I,* pp. 121–22.

the sun in Judah is as robust as a groom on the day of his marriage and as virile as an athlete about to run a race he will win.

The sun by day, as the stars at night, has the purpose of bringing glory to God. A commentary-hymn on our poem was written by another Palestinian Jew several hundred years after David wrote Psalm 19. Sirach 43:1–5 speaks of the sun as it witnesses to the wonder of God:

> The sun, when it appears, making proclamation as it goes forth,
> is a marvelous instrument, the work of the Most High. . . .
>
> Great is the Lord who made it;
> and at His command it hastens on its course.[8]

The last words produce the response God expects as we view His wonders: "Great is the Lord who made it!" Praise is due His name.

ON EXCHANGING GLORY

The stars are there by night and the sun by day. Together they witness to the glory of God. But even though they are declaring and manifesting this message constantly and universally, how many in fact receive this message rightly? Does not Paul's rebuke in his commentary on Psalm 19 suggest the answer to be very, very few? "For even though they knew God, they did not honor [glorify] Him as God, or give thanks, . . ." (Rom. 1:21ab NASB).[9]

---

[8]RSV. Sirach, or Ecclesiasticus, is one of the apocryphal books. It was written in Palestine about 180 B.C. In many ways this important book continues the wisdom tradition of the Old Testament found in such books as Proverbs and Job.

[9]The NASB text rendering is "they did not *honor* Him as God, or give thanks." The Greek verb *doxazō* is a strong New Testament word for *praise*. This is a most important text for understanding our Psalm.

The intention of God in His revelation through creation is that praise is to be given to His name. But how few respond as they ought. What usually happens is stated by Paul:

> . . . but they became futile in their speculations,
> and their foolish heart was darkened.
> Professing to be wise, they became fools, . . .
> Therefore God gave them over . . . (Rom. 1:21c,22,24a NASB).

Though natural revelation may buttress special revelation for the believer who has tuned his ear to its lovely song, countless thousands the world over and throughout time have twisted the song and have received an altogether foreign message. The stars become gods rather than witnesses to the Creator; the sun is deified rather than testifying to the Almighty. Trees are adored, mountain peaks are venerated, and the oceans are feared. For they "exchanged the glory of the incorruptible God for an image" (Rom. 1:23a), perverting the testimony of the universe that calls for His praise.

Only a believer can truly understand and enjoy creation. For only he has learned to listen to the message of its song.[10] Christians may camp outside and commune with God, but how few are the campers who praise His name. Christians may raise prize roses and glorify God, but how few are the gardeners who look beyond their own thumbs. Christians may stalk a buck in the woodlands and learn of His ways; but how few are the hunters who care for more than merely the chase, the kill, and the beer back in camp!

[10]Kidner seems to agree with this assertion. He writes, "Only the Christian is moved to filial wonder and joy at the thought of their [the heavens'] Maker." *Psalms,* vol. 1, p. 97. In a "Bulletin" from Fuller Theological Seminary, President David Allan Hubbard contrasts the Christian's proper approach to creation to that common among non-Christians, including the romantic tradition, the religious mystic tradition, the exploiters of creation. *Ecology* is basically a Christian response to God's glory expressed in creation. Hubbard says, "A human task, to put this in a word, is to care for what God has made until all his purposes are fulfilled when Christ comes again."

In creation God reveals His glory. But this message is not received rightly by many. What we need are His *words,* and these come only in His Scriptures. But when we have His words, then we learn to hear rightly the song of the heavens as well.

GOD REVEALS HIS GLORY IN HIS WORD

The transition between verses 6 and 7 in Psalm 19 seems so abrupt that some biblical scholars do not regard the Psalm as a unity. However, I find the explanation of C. S. Lewis to be most satisfactory. He notes that the key phrase of the Psalm is the line, "there is nothing hid from the heat thereof" (v. 6c KJV). That which seems to be so very different in verse 7 "hardly seems to [the psalmist] something else because it is so like the all-piercing, all-detecting sunshine."[11] The words of verse 6 serve as a subliminal connecting link in the poem. "As he has felt the sun, perhaps in the desert, searching him out in every nook of shade where he attempted to hide from it, so he feels the Law searching out all the hiding-places of his soul."[12] Here is the second section of our Psalm, verses 7–10:

(7) The instruction of Yahweh is perfect,
　　refreshing life;
　　The testimony of Yahweh is reliable,
　　making wise the simple;
(8) The directions of Yahweh are right,
　　rejoicing the heart;
　　The commandment of Yahweh is pure,
　　enlightening the eyes;
(9) The fear of Yahweh is clean,
　　enduring forever;
　　The judgments of Yahweh are truth,
　　righteous altogether.

[11]Lewis, *Reflections,* p. 64.
[12]Ibid.

(10)   They are more desirable than gold,
      even much fine gold;
    Sweeter are they than honey,
      even drippings from the comb.

Here is what the Psalm is about! We have spent much time in the first movement of Psalm 19 because of the beauty of its expression and our familiarity with its words. But the heart of the Psalm is in verses 7 through 10. R. T. France writes:

> There is a warning here: the forthright declaration that God reveals Himself to man through nature is balanced by a far higher eulogy of His revelation of Himself through His words. It is these that are the guide to right living and a true relationship with God (verses 11–14).[13]

The matchless revelation of the person of Yahweh through His written Scriptures is the proper center of this Psalm.

It is no secret that the evangelical church is presently facing a crisis of identity in terms of its commitment to the claims of Scripture about itself. Denominations, seminaries, and theologians are embroiled over the issue of the nature of Scripture.[14]

I believe that it is the teaching of this movement of the Psalm that *God reveals His glory more fully in His Word than in all of creation.* His Word corresponds with His character.

Verses 7 to 9 present a magnificently complex set of poetic parallels. These three verses have six lines of two-membered (bicola) elements. In each there is synthetic parallelism within each bicolon, but synonymous parallelism when paired with the accompanying sets. In each line of bicolon there is in the first colon a statement of the *function* of Scripture, something about what the Scripture *is*. The second

[13]R.T. France, *The Living God,* p. 30.
[14]The word *inerrancy* is used by conservative theologians to assert that the Scriptures in their original writings are without error in the whole or in the part.

gives something about what the Scripture *does*. There are six synonyms used to *denote* Scripture, six attributes used to *define* Scripture, and six excellencies used to *describe* Scripture. Further, six times the Scripture is said to be *of Yahweh*.

All of this is somewhat complicated to state, but it is delightful to enjoy. These various relationships may be seen by viewing our verses in segments.

WHAT THE SCRIPTURE IS

First, we may scan the first element of each of these lines of poetry and observe the synonyms and attributes of the Scriptures:

> The instruction of Yahweh is perfect, . . .
> The testimony of Yahweh is reliable, . . .
> The directions of Yahweh are right, . . .
> The commandment of Yahweh is pure, . . .
> The fear of Yahweh is clean, . . .
> The judgments of Yahweh are truth, . . .

As we read these elements we find six lines of synonymous parallelism. Each of these lines is saying something about the Bible that is more or less similar, but each line has its own distinctive contribution. Each may be studied by itself. But we are meant to receive the cumulative impression that all six give us together. In terms of the stereophonic model given in Chapter 4, these lines give us a true wrap-around effect with six speakers!

In another place I intend to deal with the data of these verses at some length. Here I desire only to stress three things. First, we are meant to be impressed with the recurrent use of the name *Yahweh*. In each of the six lines we are told the fact that the Scriptures are "of Yahweh." The sixfold use of the name of God is to be contrasted with the single time that the word *God* was used with reference to His revelation through creation. In creation He reveals His power, His glory, His essential deity, and His wisdom. But in His Word He reveals Himself. In His Word He reveals His triune personhood. We should never have known of God, of the Lord Jesus, of the Holy Spirit, of salvation, of heaven, of hope, of life—none of these things would we know if He had not *spoken.*

The heavens—with all of their incessant witness to God's glory—never tell of the loyal love of God. The seas—with all of their testimony of God's might—are mute concerning God's actions for Israel, His people. The trees and flowers—with all of their messages of God's wisdom—describe nothing of God's saving action in Jesus Christ, His last Word (cf. Heb. 1:1ff.). It is in the Scriptures, *and in them alone,* that we meet God as a Person. His deity and power we learn to acknowledge in what He has made. But even these factors become more clear when judged by His Word. It is really through His Word that we learn rightly how to enjoy His witness through creation.

The *second* element of these words that we should enjoy concerns the *six synonyms* for the Scriptures. The words in these verses all speak of the Scriptures, but each has its own distinctive nuance. "Instruction" ("law" in the KJV) is a picturesque word suggesting Yahweh's pointing out the road to life. Imagine yourself on a mountain trail, and you come to a crossroads. The Forest Service has placed a neatly carved sign with a pointed finger indicating the direction you are to go to reach your goal. In one sense this is the splendor of the Bible. God has, as it were, pointed out the path. We need just follow His outstretched finger.

The other terms each add their elements of the wonder of the Word. Scripture is the "testimony" of God. It is in His Word that God gives His self-authenticating revelation. His Word has behind it His will. What He authenticates is expressive of His character. The Bible is also God's "directions" and His "commandment." That is, God has the authority to speak, and He does speak. *That* He speaks is suggestive of His grace; *what* He speaks asserts His authority over our lives.

The term "fear" seems out of place in this list as a synonym for the Bible, until we realize that this phrase is to be understood as the fear in us that the Bible produces. It is a major intention of the Scriptures to produce in the believer the response of submission to His authority and majesty. The last term, "judgments," speaks of God as arbitrating in the affairs of men.

Each of these words might stand alone as descriptive of the Bible. But when they are all sounded in concert, the full impression is of the wisdom, grace, authority, and majesty of God's written revelation.

The *third* area for study in these lines of poetry is the list of six *attributes* describing the Scriptures. These lines tell us that the Scripture is "perfect, reliable, right, pure, clean, truth." These six splendors of the Bible work together to give an inescapable impression of the *quality* of Scripture as an expression of the character of God. Word studies of these several terms will display that here we have the strongest statements possible about the perfections of the Word of God. The Bible *does* claim for itself the level of integrity, truth, and purity that many are stressing today.

These words mean "free from blemish," "unpolluted," "utterly reliable," "trustworthy"—"truth" itself. Another Psalm puts it this way:

The sum of Your Word is truth,
And every one of Your righteous ordinances is everlasting (Ps. 119:160).

Or again,

For right is the Word of Yahweh,
And every work of His is truth itself (Ps. 33:4).

143

Jesus describes the Word of His Father in just the same terms:

Your Word is truth (John 17:17b).

WHAT THE SCRIPTURE DOES

The second part of each of the lines of poetry in verses 7 through 9 says something about what the Scripture does. The writers of the Bible seem never to present a theological point without then showing how that point may be applied to our living. It is not sufficient merely to set the Bible on a high pedestal for observation. The Scriptures are not to be placed on a shelf in a museum or in a display case in a jewelry store. The Scriptures *act,* for they express the will of God. Here are the elements in our Psalm:

> ... refreshing life;
> ... making wise the simple;
> ... rejoicing the heart;
> ... enlightening the eyes;
> ... enduring forever;
> ... righteous altogether.

The first five of these elements are participles in the original text, describing the ongoing, durative activity of the Scriptures. The last element is a summary statement. These several items are characteristics of the Bible.

When we read the Scriptures aright, we find refreshment that surpasses a day in the country. When we meditate in the Scriptures, we find wisdom that surpasses that gained in observing a star at night. When we study the Bible, we find a rejoicing in our heart that surpasses a walk on the seashore.

At the same time, when we read the Scriptures our experiences in the country, outside at night, or along the seashore should be enhanced. For the revelation of God in His Word, while transcending His revelation in creation, is not in opposition to it. Both work together to enrich the lives of His people.

As we look once more at these lines describing the activities of Scripture, we see that these elements are resultant from the statements about the nature of the Bible. That is, *because* "the instruction of Yahweh is perfect," we may affirm that "it refreshes life"; because "the testimony of Yahweh is reliable," we may grant that "it makes the simple wise," etc.

I well remember a fine professor of English literature who led our college class in a discussion of the difficult poem by T. S. Eliot, "The Waste Land." After a most careful analysis of the poem, its many allusions and figures, the teacher then said, "Now it is time to put all of these explanatory notes away and to read the poem for enjoyment." I wish the same for our Psalm. Turn back to the translation of the poem in this section, and let the music sing to you. With the detail in your subconsciousness, listen again to the music of these great words on the perfections of the Word of God.

A TASTE OF HONEY

It is for the reasons given in this Psalm that David then claims that there is nothing more desirable and nothing more delectable in the world than the Word of God (v. 10):

> They are more desirable than gold,
> even much fine gold;
> Sweeter are they than honey,
> even drippings from the comb.

When I was a student in Bible college, one of my teachers brought to class one day a clipping from the morning newspaper. This article described the sale of a rare Bible manuscript. It was an illustrated copy of the Book of the Revelation, a late medieval illuminated text. After quoting the price paid for this treasure, the professor asked, "I wonder if either the buyer or the seller knows that the *words* of that text are of inestimably more value than the beautiful art that has embellished the pages?" And it is true. Nothing we possess is of more value than the Bible. Today we may buy it in leather, paper, or even denim covers—it is still of great value.

Harry Golden is a Jewish commentator and philosopher of the American scene. I once heard his description of a marvelous event from his youth in New York City. His mother gathered the children into the kitchen one day for a special time. She placed their family Bible on the table. Then she got a crock of honey and a large wooden spoon. She took a dollop of honey from the crock and let it drop from the spoon onto the cover of the family Bible. Then she held the Bible before each child and asked each to lick. "Go on, lick," she said. "For I want you should never forget that this Book is sweeter than honey!" And so it is.

Before coming to Manila I thought there was nothing sweeter than honey to the taste. But after our short stay in the tropics I would like to paraphrase David's praise of the Scriptures by saying, "Sweeter are they than the mango, / even the ripe mango with the seed!"[15]

More desirable than gold and sweeter than honey, the Bible proclaims a revelation of God's glory that surpasses that of all the heavens. We are now ready for the third movement of the poem.

THE BELIEVER RESPONDS TO GOD'S GLORY

The last movement of Psalm 19 (v. 11–14) reads:

(11) Indeed your servant is warned by them,
      In keeping them there is great reward.

[15]Lewis observes that not all of us have the sweet tooth of the ancients because of our surfeit of sugar (*Reflections,* p. 63). Perhaps the Christian dental community would prefer comparison to "cool mountain water."

(12)   Errors, who can understand?
        From hidden faults acquit me.

(13)   Most of all from presumptuous ones keep Your servant,
        Let them not rule me!
        Then I shall be blameless,
        And acquitted of the great transgression.

(14) May the words of my mouth
      be according to Your desire,
  And the thoughts of my heart,
      according to Your will,
          O Yahweh, my Rock and my Redeemer.[16]

From the campfire view of the stars above, we have now come to the believer's inner being as he ponders the import of God's Scriptures in his own life. Yet notice that it is the Scriptures, not the stars, that this strophe magnifies. It is God's Word, not the heavens, that serves as our warning. It is in God's written revelation that we have great reward, not in the heat of the sun. But as the heat of the sun in Judah searches out the traveler, so the radiance of God's Word leaves nothing hidden from its searing heat. In view of the perfections of the Scriptures, the believer becomes concerned with his own sins, both hidden and presumptuous.

But when acquitted of hidden faults and kept from presumptuous ones, then God's servant is blameless and free of the "great transgression." This great sin is likely idolatry, as this would be most fitting in the theology of this Psalm.[17] It is also fitting in terms of Paul's commentary on Psalm 19 in Romans 1. Apart from the Scriptures, God's verbal revelation, people consistently misunderstand the universe, God's general revelation.

[16]At several points in this translation I am indebted to Dahood (*Psalms I,* pp. 120–125).

[17]Ibid., p. 125. Dahood compares the Hebrew phrase in this verse to a similar phrase in Gen. 20:9; Ex. 32:21,30,31; and 2 Kings 17:21. The great sin is idolatry.

For they exchanged the truth of God for [the] lie, and worshiped and served the creature rather than the Creator, who is blessed forever. Amen (Rom. 1:25 NASB).[18]

Only the believer can *truly* enjoy that which God has made, for only he has an accurate interpretation of God's creation that leads him to exultant praise of the Creator.

Finally, with the purity of God's words ringing in David's ears, he asks that his own words and thoughts be adequate and pleasing to Yahweh:

> May the words of my mouth
>   be according to Your desire,
> And the thoughts of my heart
>   according to Your will,
>   O Yahweh, my Rock and my Redeemer!

THE GRAND SWEEP

From the stars above to the Scriptures in hand and then to the human soul—such has been the sweep of this grand Psalm.

One of the leading Old Testament scholars in America in the last generation was Dr. E. J. Young of Westminster. At his death on February 18, 1968, his longtime friend Dr. John Murray wrote a stirring tribute. He spoke of Young's humility, consistency, tireless labor, mastery of languages, and evidence of the fruit of the Spirit in his life. But most of all Murray praised Young for his dedication to the Scriptures. "He burned with holy jealousy for the integrity of God's Word and for the maintenance of the whole counsel of God."[19]

[18]This follows the marginal reading in the NASB. "The lie" seems to reflect "the great crime" of our Psalm.

[19]Found in the publisher's preface to E.J. Young, *In the Beginning: Genesis Chapters 1 to 3 and the Authority of Scripture* (Edinburgh: Banner of Truth, 1976), p. 7.

Then Murray wrote:

> The distinction for which, above all others, Dr. Young should be commended and remembered as a scholar is the reverence he entertained for Scripture as the Word of God. To the defense of the Bible as such, and to its exposition as the living Word of the living God, he devoted all his talents and energies. The Bible he believed was revelation from God, always relevant and by the Holy Spirit sealed in our hearts to be what it intrinsically is, the inerrant Word of God.[20]

Dr. Young learned well the song of Psalm 19!

If we are ever to learn to praise Yahweh, it will be because we have learned of Him through the purity of His great Word, and then have learned how to enjoy Him rightly through all that He has made.

The next time you are sitting in front of a campfire with your eyes on the stars, let your eyes go back to His Word before the fire dies out!

[20]Ibid., p. 8.

CHAPTER 10

Psalm 13
When God Seems Far Away

Then the waters would have engulfed us,
The torrent would have swept over our being;
Then would have swept over our being
The insolent waters.

—Psalm 124:4,5

Probably our greatest question respecting praise is how to manage when life is rough and God seems far away. How do we praise Him then? Psalm 13 is an intensely moving Psalm of lament that sets an example of how to cope when life is strained and praise is a forgotten impulse. To appreciate this Psalm in its emotional intensity, it is necessary to set a mood and sustain it, a mood of loneliness and despair.

THROUGH A GLASS, COLDLY

Winter has gripped the land, and so strong is its hold that the land has ceased to struggle. The variegated colors of fall are forgotten, and the splendors of the recent summer are gone. All is lost of color and life with winter now in complete control.

An elderly woman is sitting in her rocking chair with her shawl wrapped tightly around her frail form. She sits and rocks and gazes out her frosted window pane onto her frozen fields. A sense of melancholy drapes itself over her already burdened shoulders. She senses somehow that her life is very much like the scene before her in winter's icy grip.

For her, as for her fields—color, vitality, and energy have all been smothered out. She senses that what winter's cold compress has done outside, so time and life have done to her within.

Her problem is that she is all alone. And her loneliness is to her like winter's cold breath. She adjusts her shawl . . . and rocks.

The nights are worse. Sometimes, she awakens with a start and reaches over for that familiar form, but she finds the covers are unnaturally smooth. Herby has been gone now for nine years.

She is alone, and she is forgotten. So forgotten does she feel that down deep she sighs that perhaps *even God* has forgotten her.

What is your reaction to the charge that God has forgotten? Do you rush to say that all that God forgets is the believers' sins, that He casts them into the depths of the sea (see Mic. 7:19) and, as Corrie ten Boom says with a twinkle in her eye, "He posts a sign that says, 'No Fishing' "? Or, perhaps, you seize on the word "forget" and say, "But that is something people do!" Then you recount some "great forgetters" that you have known.

One of my beloved professors once spoke at a week-long series of meetings in a city a few hundred miles from his home. After the week was over, he flew back to his own city, took a cab to his home, and was greeted at the door by his questioning wife: "But where is the car? Did you forget that you drove this time?" He had forgotten! He had to take a taxi back to the airport, fly to the other city, and drive his forgotten car home!

Forgetfulness is a "people-kind-of-thing." It is not a unique trait of the absentminded professor. We all forget at times. Is it also possible, if even for a moment, that *God* may forget? Might He forget His own? When this question is asked intently, then all the fun of the absentminded professor is lost. What horror replaces the humor! What do we do *when God forgets?* This is likely not a new question for us.

None of us can explain adequately the tragedies that happen to tens, scores—even thousands—in remote places on our troubled earth. But do we not sometimes wonder, in the pagan's litany: "If there were a God, would these things happen?" Does God forget?

Perhaps the question is more pointed when we think of an individual, rather than of the troubled masses. In my first interim pastorate there was a family that was given an inordinate amount of suffering. The young mother of four children was a lovely woman whose heart was full of love for God. Then she was stricken with a terrible viral infection that settled in her brain. She was hospitalized for months and had numerous tests and operations. Her husband, troubled with her ailment—and the family's mounting medical bills—was himself hospitalized for a time because of nerve-induced hives.

While I was visiting this young woman one night, she looked at me with a face distorted from medication, her hair shaved off for the next morning's surgery, her body wasting, and her heart troubled for her children and her home. She held my hand, looked into my eyes, and asked a question I will never forget: "Pastor, *has God forgotten me?*"

When these words come from one of God's children, they cannot be shrugged off easily. Whether it comes from an old woman in a cold room, a young mother in a hospital bed, a father with a dying child, or an old man with a lost hope, the question is real, persistent, and nagging. Can the God of knowledge have a memory block? Can the only wise God be absentminded? Is it possible that the Omniscient can forget, even for a moment, one of His children?

For an answer to this question, I wish to take you back again to the Book of Psalms where so often we find *our very feelings* reflected in words we may not yet have dared to use but which are exactly the words we wish! The passage is Psalm 13, "the Psalm of a forgetting God."

HOW LONG?

This little poem has three movements to it, each of two verses. The first movement may be rendered as follows:

> To the choir director.
> A Psalm of David.

(1) How long, O Yahweh?
   Will You forget me forever?
   How long—
   will You hide Your face from me?
(2) How long—
   shall I take counsel within,
   yet having sorrow in my heart all the day?
   How long—
   will my enemy be exalted over me?

Listen again to the fourfold chant, "How long?" Read the words aloud, slowly and with feeling. Do you hear their pain, their plaintive cry? Can you read these words several times and not be caught up with them? In awful repetition the psalmist chants: "How long, how long, how long, how long?"[1]

These are the impassioned words of one who believes him-

[1]The fourfold "how long" has parallels in Babylonian laments. Sabourin quotes from a Babylonian prayer of lamentation to the goddess Ishtar where a fourfold "how long?" is found, including this very similar line: "How long, O my lady, wilt thou be infuriated so that thy love is turned away?" The full poem is found in *Ancient Near Eastern Texts Relating to the Old Testament,* ed. J.B. Pritchard, 2nd. ed. (Princeton: Princeton University Press, 1969), pp. 383–84.

self truly forgotten by God. The statement underlying the question in this Psalm is even more terrifying. The substructural issue is not *can* God forget, but He *has* forgotten! The psalmist raises a more difficult question, based on the reasoning of fear: Since God has forgotten, and since God is eternal, *does His forgetfulness last forever?* Hence, the somber, fourfold "how long?"

In awful synonymous parallelism to the words, "How long will You forget me?" is the stark question, "How long will You hide Your face from me?" It is as though, in picture language, the psalmist describes God not merely with His attention elsewhere, but deliberately avoiding the believer.

The point of the first movement of this Psalm is to suggest that there may come, even in the life of the believer, the feeling that God has forgotten. David said, long before our experiences in life, "God has forgotten; God has turned away."

In the structure of the Psalms of lament,[2] these words form the "You" element of the lament proper. As we have seen earlier in our survey of Psalm 6, the lament often has three pronouns expressing distress: *I* am hurting, *You* (God) do not care, and *they* (the enemy) are winning. So in this Psalm the "You" factor is prominent. You, God, have forgotten; You, God have turned away.

Since he believes he is forgotten by God, David turns to his own resources, only to be frustrated again and again. In the "I" element of the lament, in compressed poetry, David seems to suggest that he lies awake at night, trying to find some escape, some way out of his troubles.[3] But the coming of light, which should bring new hope, only renews his pain, and he has another day of sorrow in his heart ahead of him. His plans

[2]You may wish to review again the introduction to the Psalms of lament in Chapter 3. There Psalm 6 was used as an example.

[3]Kidner speaks of "a turmoil of thought (cf. 77:36) rather than the dull ache of dejection." *Psalms,* vol. 1, p. 77.

are futile plans; his counsel is worthless counsel. He is hurting, and he knows no way out.

All the while, like slow, circling vultures, his enemies hover above, waiting for his fall—and their meal! The last of the four "how longs" relates to the "they" element of the lament:

How long—
    will my enemy be exalted over me?

It is not necessary to try to identify this enemy, nor to try to place this Psalm within a known, specific time in David's life.[4] The very lack of specificity helps us to identify with this Psalm. His enemy is our enemy; his distress is our distress. And yes, at times, even his complaint to God may be found on our lips.

But one curious item remains. There is a break of logic of a sort. If it is really true that God has forgotten, then *why pray?* If it is really true that God has turned away, then *why even bother?* This hiatus is intensified when we observe that David's initial cry is addressed, "O Yahweh!" David is using the name of relationship as he laments God's lack of faith! But still he prays.

On this confusing, but all-too-familiar human pattern, Martin Luther once wrote, "Our hope despairs, and our despair yet hopes." Finally we must leave our praying to the Spirit whose groaning on our behalf is beyond our comprehension. Nevertheless, the first section of this little Psalm

---

[4]Dahood (*Psalms I,* pp. 77–78) suggests the enemy to be death, more specifically *Mot,* the Canaanite god of death and sterility. The plural "adversaries" (v. 4) he takes as a plural of majesty ("my Adversary"). Sabourin (*Psalms,* pp. 223–24) gives some assent to this view. In my own approach I am taking the enemy more generally and figuratively. Kidner states, "Awareness of God and the enemy is virtually the hallmark of every psalm of David; the positive and the negative charge which produced the driving-horse of his best years" (*Psalms,* vol. 1, p. 78).

presents the sobering thought: Even a believer may feel at times that God has forgotten or abandoned him.

THEN WE SHOULD PRAY

The second movement of this Psalm serves as an integral transition between the lament of verses 1 and 2 and the praise of verses 5 and 6. This central section is the *petition*. It may be read as follows:

> (3) Consider me! Answer me![5]
>   O Yahweh my God!
>   Enlighten my eyes,
>   Lest I sleep the sleep of death;
> (4) Lest my enemy say, "I have overcome him";
>   Lest my adversaries rejoice when I am shaken.

Here we have in classic format the elements of the petition. There is a scream to God to *hear,* followed by a call for Him to *save.* (The third element, to *punish,* is lacking in this Psalm, though the enemies are prominent.) When we get into a true spiritual "down" period, so that we even begin to doubt God, *then we must pray* beseechingly for God to hear and to save.

I recognize that for some people the advice, "Pray about it," seems trite. For others the giving of these words may be an easy out for the real act of caring. But it is still true that if this direction is given in sincerity and compassion, and if it is received as it is given, then it is the best advice that can ever be proffered for a hurting brother or sister.

Notice how David, in an economy of expression, intensifies his prayer by adding the words, "O Yahweh my God!" This is his *confession of trust.* It is given even in the midst of his despair. The God who has forgotten him is the only God there

[5]The suffix on the first verb is supplied by the double-duty suffix on the second verb.

is. Yahweh, who has turned His back, is Yahweh alone. To whom else can we turn? It is always true that only He has life-giving words.

David buttresses his prayer by *motifs of motivation* to compel God to respond. There are three, and they are found in verses 3 and 4. David says that if God does not answer his prayer, he will die. Not only will this be the death of one of God's servants, David states, but also his enemy will believe that he has won the victory.

The implication of these words, in a polytheistic world, is that the enemy's god[6] (who is no god) will have prevailed over Yahweh (who is God alone). Here, David's case becomes one of vindicating the character of God. Moreover, he concludes, all his adversaries will rejoice when he is shaken. For they too will assume the perverse pride of paganism at the fall of one who has stood for the living God. This will give the unrepentant more excuse to justify their perfidy.

These motifs of motivation ought to be instructional for us in our own prayers, as well as in our teaching of children to pray. The results of God's response should be thought out to help determine the worthiness of the request. Why should not a three-year-old pray for a "Hershey bar as big as her backyard"? Well, in part, because her parents might have to sell that backyard to pay off the consequent doctor and dental bills! We who are more mature still are found on occasion to have rather infantile requests—requests which, if thought out, would never need to have been uttered.

ACQUAINTED WITH DEATH

After looking at the motivational elements, we now need to see more exactly what David's petition was. The *save* petition

[6]In Dahood's view (see note 4, above), it is not the enemy's god, but a competing deity in *David's* life (*Mot,* the god of death and sterility). I reject this approach for it leaves us with the uneasy feeling that David was drinking too deeply from the cup of polytheism himself.

of his prayer is, in fact, a bit puzzling when we first read it. The request is "enlighten my eyes!" (v. 3b).

This poem is so very brief, and its emotional level is so highly intense, that it is difficult to be confident of each implication. Yet, I wish to suggest that David is here using an image from his long career as a frontline soldier. David had long experienced hand-to-hand combat. In his day there were no heroic medics who would rush a fallen comrade to a waiting helicopter that would fly him to modern medical care.

In David's army, when a man fell, he would likely remain fallen until the battle was over, with the hot Palestinian soil drinking his life juices away. Then, at the end of the day, with each army back in its own camp, there might be those who would pick up the fallen, press out their wounds, apply bandages, and mollify them with herbs and olive oil (see Is. 1:6). Such rudimentary medical care would not meet with a high level of success after the carnage wrought by swords, spears, arrows, and axes, or the even more terrifying weapons of the siege machines and chariots—the heavy artillery and tanks of the ancient world.

David was well acquainted with death, particularly that brought about by ghastly battle wounds. Surely he had cradled the heads of fallen friends on his lap and heard their last words.

David compares himself to one who is about to die. For he, like fallen comrades before him, speaks of failing eyesight— an ominous premonition of the end. When David screams:

> Enlighten my eyes,
>   lest I sleep the sleep of death;

he is using the imagery of a slowly dying man whose life forces are fading. Unless Yahweh were to restore his eyes, he would soon be dead.[7]

---

[7]Over a century ago the great commentator Franz Delitzsch wrote: "To lighten the eyes that are dimmed with sorrow and ready to break, is equiva-

It is hard to imagine a more brilliant image than this to convey the truth of this Psalm. I believe that David is suggesting that the problem of a forgetting God is *in our view of Him.* When we feel that God has forgotten us, then we need Him to answer our prayer, which we learned to pray from God's servant David: "Enlighten my eyes!"

We need to have our eyes refocused on the character of our God. The spiritual cataracts must be removed. No more fitting image could David have used than this one. In those times when we feel that God is forgetting us, we need to pray for a new view of Him.

The first part of this Psalm suggests that there may come a time when it seems that God has forgotten. The second movement urges the believer to pray for an enlightening of his eyes, for a new perspective of His God.

This transitional movement of the Psalm prepares us for the third section of the poem.

THEN WE SHALL REMEMBER

Verses 5 and 6 of our Psalm could not present a stronger contrast with the mood of the preceding section. These verses read:

(5) But I, in Your loyal love, I trust;
   My heart shall rejoice in Your salvation.
(6) I will sing to Yahweh,
   Because He will have dealt bountifully with me.

---

lent to, empart new life (Ezra ix. 8), which is reflected in the fresh clear brightness of the eye (1 Sam. xiv. 27, 29). The lightning light, to which (this verb) points, is the light of love beaming from the divine countenance, xxxi. 17. He, upon whom God looks down in love, continues in life, new powers of life are imparted to him, it is not his lot to sleep the death, *i.e.* the sleep of death, Jer. li. 39, 57, cf. Ps. lxxvi.6." Franz Delitzsch, *Biblical Commentary on the Psalms,* vol. 1, pp. 200–201.

The change of mood is noticed first in the phrase, "But I," in verse 5a.[8] This is the signal for a distinct change in mood. The only explanation is that God has answered the prayer of David. He has "enlightened his eyes" by providing a new view of His character.

In the Old Testament period we may presume that such an enlightenment would have come from a priest or a prophet. A new revelation would have come to David in direct response to his prayer. He has not yet, in fact, been delivered from his trouble, for his praise is still future (vv. 5b,6). Nevertheless, he has learned a new level of trusting response to Yahweh in adversity.

In our own day of distress it would be a mistake to look for a *new* revelation of God from a priest, a prophet, or any other source. For we have a complete revelation in the Scriptures of God, something David had only in part. We need not new words, but a new insight into and a fresh understanding of the *old* words. Our problem often is not a lack of revelation, but a failure to appropriate the revelation we have. For this reason, though, when we pray David's prayer ("enlighten my eyes"), we expect a slightly different response. We look for a new level, or a fresh reminder, or a new understanding in the Scriptures of God.

So where does that lead us? It leads us back to the *old answers:* in adversity (as well as in blessing), "Pray and read the Bible!" As simple as that? As corny as that? Well, it is *not* simple. And it is only a cliché if given—or received—on a superficial level. If prayer is truly regarded as communication with Deity, and if the Bible is genuinely believed to be the revelation of God in written words—then there can be no more profound advice this side of glory than to do just these things in faith: pray and read the Scriptures!

[8]Westermann writes, "At the place where the change in the mood of the psalmist occurs, almost all of these Psalms contains a *Waw* adversative, 'But thou O God . . . ,' or 'But I . . .' " (*Praise of God,* p. 70). The Hebrew letter *waw* may be a copulative "and" or an adversative "but."

THEN WE REMEMBER

These, in effect, are the steps David took. As we have seen him go through this process, we recognize reality, not corn; profound truth, not cliché. In those times when we feel that God is forgetting us, those are the times *we need to remember Him!* It turns out that forgetting *is* a "people-kind-of-thing" after all.

David says, "But I, in Your loyal love, I trust" (v. 5a). In these words the same David that charged God with being forgetful himself remembers. David remembers one of the grandest characteristics of Yahweh displayed in the Psalms: His loyal love. The point of this whole Psalm hinges on the Hebrew word *ḥesed,* the loyal love of Yahweh. The teaching of the Psalm is that *in Yahweh's loyal love there is no forgetting.*

It seems that the Spirit, knowing *our* tendencies, allowed David to challenge this basic aspect of God's character, only to have his challenge refuted and his faith strengthened in the loyal love of God. It is through the catharsis of suffering that David's stand of faith in Yahweh's essential loving loyalty is strengthened.

We sometimes speak of a threshold of pain. Perhaps we might also speak of a threshold of faith. When our faith is put through testing, and God brings us through that test, we are then ready to believe Him more intensely than ever before. Abraham on Mount Moriah (see Gen. 22) is the Old Testament example of this concept without parallel.[9] Jesus is the supreme example in the New Testament. The writer to the Hebrews reports:

> In the days of His flesh, when He offered up both prayers and
> supplications with loud crying and tears to Him who was able
> to save Him from death, and who was heard because of His

[9]It was in Genesis 22 that Abraham's faith was tested by God supremely as he was told to sacrifice his son Isaac. This narrative is one of the most dramatic and touching chapters in all of Genesis.

piety, although He was a Son, *He learned obedience from the things which He suffered* (Heb. 5:7,8 NASB, emphasis added).

There is thus a continuity of learning faithful obedience through suffering from Abraham—through Job, David, and scores of Old Testament believers—culminating in the person of Jesus Christ. It is difficult to accept this truth at the time of our own suffering. But when we are allowed by God to stretch our threshold of faith through suffering, we are made a part of the most illustrious company of all time.

So it was that through this experience David learned anew and more deeply the reality of the loyal love of God. He speaks of this excellence of Yahweh many times in many Psalms. It seems as though this characteristic of God, which is most wonderful, is something one has to have a growing confidence in, and in which there is to be a developing appreciation. We keep coming back to this, one of the most central attributes of God. It is the loyal love of God that the Psalms regularly present for our praise.

GOD AND MOTHERS

Later in Israel's history, an entire generation experienced what David felt. They also sensed that they were abandoned by God. They sensed that they were forgotten by the One who does not forget. Into the mouth of that generation, the prophet Isaiah was led to put these words:

But Zion said, "Yahweh has forsaken me,
And the Lord has forgotten me" (Is. 49:14).

Here it is again; the old charge is said anew. On this occasion, however, God Himself responded with a rhetorical question:

"Is it possible that a woman forget her nursing child,
And cease to have compassion on a son born of her
womb?" (Is. 49:15ab).

We would say, "No. God has built within a mother such a
capacity for love for her child that she could never forget nor
cease to care for her child." Of such noble thoughts are
Mothers' Day greeting cards made. Fathers may be fickle, but
not mothers!

But the Bible is not sentimental in a self-deceptive way.
There are mothers who, for twisted and tormented reasons
within them that they likely do not understand, have indeed
forgotten, abandoned—and even destroyed—children they
nursed, sons and daughters of their wombs.

I worked for several years as a group-worker in the Dallas
County Detention Home in Texas, working on the graveyard
shift. While it was not a part of our regular duties, there were
times when we admitted children for the night who had not
committed crimes but against whom terrible wrongs had
been done. These acts had been committed at times by fathers
or mothers. Sometimes these children were beaten, abandoned, starved, or abused in indescribable ways. After treatment at the county medical center, they might be brought to
our facility until a foster home could be found the next day.

It is the implied point of God's question that the answer
should be "No, never!" But, in fact, the answer is "Sometimes,
yes." For He concludes:

"Ah, even these may forget;
But as for Me, I am unable to forget you" (v. 15c).

"Look," He says, "your names are inscribed on my palms!"
(v. 16a). We have an expression "to know someone as well as
the palm of one's hand." In the case of God, that is our position
with Him.

God has so closely related Himself to the believer that His character is at stake (even as David implied), should He ever, even for a moment, cease to think and care for His own. What even a mother may forget, He cannot forget. His lovebond surpasses the deepest affection level known among mankind: The love a mother has for her child. He cannot forget His own.[10]

IN LOYAL LOVE THERE IS NO FORGETTING

When we say that God is eternal, we mean that He cannot die. When we say that God is truth, we mean that He cannot lie. And when we say that God loves His people with loyal love, we mean that with all of His power notwithstanding, *He cannot forget* those who are His. "For He cannot deny Himself!" (2 Tim. 2:13 NASB). God loves His people with loyal love, and *in loyal love there is no forgetting.*

For this reason, David ends in *song* the poem he began with a sob. While still not out of his distress, he knows that one day he will complete his vow of praise:

My heart shall rejoice in your salvation!
I will sing to Yahweh,
Because He will have dealt bountifully with me!
(vv. 5b,6).

By these words of oath, David pledges to his loyal Lord that when he is delivered he will go before the congregation of the faithful and praise God for His deliverance. He will tell the community that God brought him out, even though he had thought that God had forgotten him.

My father, Barclay Allen, was a nationally known musician in the forties. He lay in a bed for seventeen years,

[10]The verb in Isaiah 49:15c is an imperfect of possibility, stated in the negative.

however, following a terrible accident that left him paralyzed from the neck down. This accident in 1949 was used by God to bring my father in due time to a saving knowledge of the Lord Jesus Christ.

Yet, even though my father knew the Lord, there were times of great discouragement and periods of intense pain. For many of those years he could not exercise his unusual musical abilities. Quite honestly and frankly, there were times he could have sung the first line of David's Psalm of lament and done so in a most minor key indeed:

How long, O Yahweh—
Will You forget me forever?

Pressures built on my mother as well. There were periods when she might have joined in sad harmony the second line:

How long—
will You hide your face from me?

And yet, our Lord in His perfect compassion took my father home to join Him in His forever in November 1966. At that time my father entered the glory of his Father. Then there was no "snapping of the fingers" in belated recognition, no "wrinkling of the brow of Deity" in puzzlement—such is blasphemous even to think! When my father was brought before his Lord, all heaven exulted in what we are learning: God loves His people with loyal love, and *there just can be no forgetting in the loyal love of Yahweh.*

For this we praise Your name, our great God!

CHAPTER 11

Psalm 138
Why Pray?

> Is anyone among you suffering?
> Let him pray.
> Is anyone cheerful?
> Let him sing psalms.
>   —James 5:13, NKJB

"Men ought always to pray." This is the clear teaching of our Lord (see Luke 18:1 KJV). It is taught in concert with the whole of Scripture. We are taught this, we read it, and we believe it, . . . yet at times we ask the question, "Why?"

Why should we pray? Does God need our prayer to aid Him in directing the affairs of the universe? Does the Almighty need our instruction for His work? Does the Omniscient need our suggestions to be placed in His "heavenly box"? Why pray? Would not His will be done even if we did not pray for it? Even though Jesus commands us to pray, sometimes we wonder "Why?"

THE PURPOSE OF PRAYER

I wish to present a Psalm in which the *reason* for prayer is given in such a way that it ought to outweigh all of our inadequate feelings based on weak moments in our own prayer life. Psalm 138 is a dramatic Davidic hymn in which prayer is connected vitally with praise. Simply stated, this

Psalm declares: *The purpose of prayer is to glorify God.* There are many other things that may be said about prayer, but I know of no truth more profound, more far-reaching, or more significant about prayer than this: *Prayer glorifies God!*

Following the lead of this Psalm we might speak of prayer and praise as a spiritual plant. Prayer is the rootage of that plant, and praise is the flower. When we pray—not foolishly, not in a silly manner, not in a shallow way—but intensely, fervently, and dependently, God answers. And our response to His answer is to give praise to His name. *This* is why we pray. We pray so that when He answers us, we may renew our praise to His glory.

THE STRUCTURE OF PSALM 138

David's Psalm on the purpose of prayer, Psalm 138, has three movements to it, as we have found in several of these poems. These three strophes may be seen by a careful observation of the internal structure. In verses 1 to 3 David is praising God in the first person ("I will praise You"). In verses 4 to 6 David projects a future praise of God by the kings of the earth ("they will praise You"). Finally, in verses 7 and 8 David reflects on his own continuing walk of dependent prayer to God ("even though I walk").

PRAISE FOR ANSWERED PRAYER

In the first movement of this Psalm David praises God for *an extraordinary answer to his prayer* (vv. 1–3). That which he emphasizes in this Psalm is not his prayer, but God's answer to it. This poem is a Psalm of declarative praise. That is, it is a Psalm of praise to God for that which He has done for the believer. *Praise is in response* to God's great answer.

Here are the words of the first movement:

(1) Of David.
    I acknowledge You with all my heart;
    Before gods I sing Your praises!
(2) I prostrate myself to Your holy temple,
    And I acknowledge Your name—
        according to Your loyal love
        and according to Your steadfastness—
    For You have magnified above all Your name Your
        word!
(3) When I called, You answered me.
    You have emboldened me with strength within!

In this translation there are several major interpretational issues before us. In the detail that follows, however, we should not lose sight of the major truth of this first movement: David gives God great praise for an extraordinary answer to his prayer.

I WILL TELL YOUR NAME

The first major issue concerns the nature of praise. In this Psalm the key word for praise is the Hebrew word *yādāh*. Although translated by the English verb "to praise" in the KJV in the first verse ("I will praise thee with my whole heart"), it has become customary to render this word by "to give thanks," such as is in the NASB ("I will give Thee thanks with all my heart").

The basic meaning of this key term for praise is "to give public acknowledgment." The KJV is far nearer the intent of this verb in Psalm 138 than some modern translations. As mentioned earlier, in the Old Testament culture one "gave thanks" to God by *telling others* about His character or His benevolence. It is in this public declaration that Yahweh's name is praised.[1]

[1]The world of the Old Testament differs so much from our cultures, respecting the lack of a word for "thank," that it is difficult for us to imagine such a

After saying something about this issue in a church in British Columbia, I was approached by an elderly gentleman who wished a word with me. He gave me his card and introduced himself as a veteran medical missionary to India. He had established a medical mission in a region where progressive blindness was endemic, where thousands of people were born sighted but were doomed to blindness as they matured.

In a marvelous ministry to the whole man, this ophthalmologist had developed a procedure to arrest the terrible disease that had ravaged the people of that region. He then told me that as people would leave that clinic knowing that they would see, when otherwise they might have become blind, they would not say "thank you," for that was not in their dialect. Instead they would say, "I will tell your name!"

This is precisely what we have in the Old Testament. We learn to praise God by giving proclamation to His name. This is just what David declares: *"I acknowledge You* with all my heart!"[2]

David states his intention to praise Yahweh in verse 1 without yet declaring his reason. He does declare his personal involvement, however, in words that are characteristic of the Psalms: "with all my heart." Genuine praise can never be

[2]Some manuscripts have a different reading for this colon. They add the name of God, Yahweh, so that it reads: "I acknowledge You, O Yahweh, with all my heart." Further, the Septuagint (the ancient translation of the Hebrew Scripture into Greek) reads an additional colon: "For You have heard the words of my mouth." We judge the first addition to be unnecessary, as the one addressed is quite clear. The Greek reading, which is in accord with the theology of the Psalm, is to be rejected also because it detracts from the suspense of the Psalm. We are not told until verse 3 the reason for David's great praise of God.

situation *unless* we realize that public acknowledgment took the place of the giving of thanks. Westermann writes, "We are compelled to imagine a world in which petition plays a thoroughly essential and noteworthy role, but where the opposite role of petition is not primarily thanks but praise. And this praise is a stronger, more likely, broader concept which includes our 'thanks' in it. Thanking is here included entirely within praise." *Praise of God,* p. 25.

external or flippant, never superficial or frivolous. It must involve one's whole being. As David puts it in Psalm 103:1:

> Bless Yahweh, O my being;
> And all within me bless His holy name.

BEFORE THE GODS

A second major interpretational issue in the first movement of this Psalm concerns the concept of praise made before the gods. David says, "I will sing praises to You before the gods." This concept is found in all English editions except the *Living Bible* which reads, "before angels."[3]

Many people ask why "the gods" would be brought into this Psalm of praise. Perhaps we have not taken seriously enough the polytheistic context of the Old Testament world. David, who was a strict monotheist, lived in a world convinced of polytheism. The belief in many gods permeated the ancient Near East. This destructive belief was, moreover, a constant threat to Israel throughout her history prior to the Babylonian captivity.

I believe that when David says, "I will sing praises to You before the gods!" he is asserting a frontal attack on the paganism all about him. God has so dramatically answered his prayer that (as he is to say in verse 3b) he is newly emboldened within and ready for a confrontation.

David knew that all about him people were giving sacrifice and praise to gods who were not, to deities who are not, and to idols who will not ever exist. Against them all he sings in bold song to Yahweh who was, and is, and ever shall be (as His name demands). This is praise in enemy territory.

[3]The Living Bible here follows the Septuagint. That the Hebrew word for "gods" may not refer in fact to *God* (as some have suggested) is clear from the grammar of the line. The word "gods" follows a preposition ("before"), and prepositions in Hebrew always govern the genitive case. The translation must be "before the gods." "Before You, O God" would call for another Hebrew construction.

In this Psalm David anticipates the New Testament imperative, "Go and tell,"[4] for he has been so emboldened that he declares his intent to sing the praises of God before those who do not know Him.

IN THE GATHERING OF THE SAINTS

The second verse continues David's determined exaltation of God:

I prostrate myself toward Your holy temple,
And I acknowledge Your name—
    according to Your loyal love
    and according to Your steadfastness—
For You have magnified above all Your name Your word.

This verse begins with a regular expression of the setting of praise, the congregation in the precincts of the tabernacle or temple.[5] Psalm 149 speaks of singing the praise of Yahweh "in the gathering of the saints" (v. 1), accompanied by dance and instrumental music (v. 3).

Similarly, Psalm 111 has the setting of praise "in the assembly of the upright, even the congregation" (v. 1). David in

[4]George W. Peters, *A Biblical Theology of Missions* (Chicago: Moody, 1972), speaks of a *centripetal* motion in the missions of the Old Testament, a movement from the outside into the center. This is expressed by the words, "Taste and see that the LORD is good" (Ps. 34:8). In the New Testament, missions becomes a *centrifugal* force, movement from the inside out: "Go and tell." This latter is the essence of the Great Commission texts (Matt. 28:18-27; Acts 1:8; Luke 24:46-48, and perhaps Mark 16:15). See pp. 19-25 and the chart on p. 22 of his book.

[5]The term "temple" need not imply that this is a post-Davidic Psalm. The sanctuary at Shiloh (cf. 1 Sam. 1:3) had ceased to be a mere tent earlier in Israel's history. During the reign of David the ark was brought to Jerusalem (2 Sam. 6:12–18), and, while lacking a splendid setting, could still be called a "temple" (but, cf., 7:2). See J.J. Stewart Perowne, *The Book of Psalms,* 2 vols. (London: George Bell and Sons, 1879), vol. 2, p. 435; cf. Kidner, *Psalms,* vol. 1, pp. 59,121.

our present Psalm assumes a posture of obeisance toward the temple in the midst of the congregation.

In praise David extols God who has acted in concert with His character. This is what he means by the words "according to your loyal love and according to your steadfastness" (v. 2b). God has magnified His name in accordance with His character.

This is a regular motivation for praise, as we have seen in earlier chapters. When you and I have experienced something great in response to prayer, we *need* to seize the opportunity to share these experiences with the congregation. We will be strengthened when we share with others what God has done for us. The community as a whole will be strengthened as well. Our words will find response in other people. They will be prompted to share in turn. From one believer to another, the glory of God may reverberate through the congregation. Glory will be added to glory; His name will be resounded in praise; His people will be excited and refreshed—such is the wonder of true praise in the community.

ABOVE YOUR WORD?

The last words of verse 2 present a third interpretational issue in this Psalm. The words, "For You have magnified above all Your name Your word," seem to defy all analogy. From ancient times interpreters have struggled with this text. From the Septuagint, which reads, "You have magnified Your holy name above all," to the NASB, which reads, "For Thou hast magnified Thy word according to all Thy name," translators have attempted to soften the impact of the original wording.

These words seem to suggest that God's *word* is more important than His *name*. This is manifestly inconceivable. For if the name Yahweh is a summary of the reality of God, how may anything be more important? This verse cannot refer to the Bible, as has been suggested by some writers. No matter how highly we may reverence God's Scriptures, we may not exalt His Word over Himself. The Scriptures reveal God's glory, as Psalm 19 declares. But the Scriptures may not be said to transcend God's glory.[6] The difficulty of these words is genuine, but in dealing with it we should attempt to come to grips with the clear wording of the Hebrew text.

I suggest that by the term "word," David is referring not to the Bible but to *the specific answer to prayer* he mentions in verse 3. He is not speaking of the Scriptures as a whole, but of a specific and concrete revelation that he has received from God. This revelation was so surprising in its comprehensiveness, so unexpected in its fullness, that David ecstatically declares that what he learned of Yahweh through this experience transcended all that he knew of Him beforehand. This prior knowledge he summarizes as "Your name."

For these reasons verses 1 to 3 present David praising God for an extraordinary answer to his prayer. This wholly unexpected answer came even as David prayed and gave him a new courageousness based on God's goodness:

> When I called, You answered me;
> You have emboldened me with new inner courage (v. 3).

This splendid affirmation suggests several New Testament passages on the wonder of prayer. One concerns the surprise of faith as God's answer exceeds our fondest hope. Paul praised God for this reason in these words:

---

[6]Such would really be "bibliolatry" as Kidner warns (*Psalms,* vol. 2, p. 462). The point of view that I am presenting was anticipated by Perowne (*Psalms,* vol. 2, p. 436). Kidner himself follows the emendation proposed in the RSV (and the NASB margin) that the letter *w* meaning "and" had been dropped by a copyist. He suggests the reading: "For Thou has exalted above everything Thy name and Thy word" (vol. 2, p. 462). There seems to be no manuscript evidence for this approach, however.

Now to Him who is able to do exceeding abundantly beyond all that we ask or think, according to the power that works within us, to Him be the glory in the church and in Christ Jesus to all generations forever and ever. Amen (Eph. 3:20,21 NASB).

The extraordinary nature of God's answers to our prayers expands our view of His greatness. This leads us to glorify His name, and *such is the purpose of prayer.*

Another New Testament passage is prompted by the wording of verse 3a of our Psalm, "When I called you answered me." In our requests we do not surprise God or bring Him news! As Jesus instructed His disciples who desired to pray correctly, God's people should avoid meaningless repetition in prayer. We are to remember Jesus' words: "Your Father knows what you need, before you ask Him. . . . for your heavenly Father knows that you need all these things" (Matt. 6:8b,32b NASB). Before we ask, He is already at work on His knowing response!

Again, the wording of verse 3b ("You have emboldened me with new inner courage") suggests the holy boldness we may have in prayer as believers in the risen Jesus, our great High Priest. The writer to the Hebrews urges us to pray this way in these words: "Since therefore, brethren, we have confidence to enter the holy place by the blood of Jesus, . . . let us draw near with a sincere heart in full assurance of faith" (Heb. 10:19, 22a NASB).

Despite the three major interpretational issues that the first strophe of this Psalm presents to us, the intention of the first three verses remains clear. David praises God for an answer to prayer that overwhelmed him. In his praise he gives God public acknowledgment. David extends his praise of God into enemy territory as he dares to sing of Yahweh "before the gods" in bold witness. Finally, David describes his answer to prayer to be beyond all that he previously had known of God. David's praise to God is thus unrestrained.

If the purpose of prayer is to bring us to the praise of God, it may be that the reason we fail to praise God lies in our failure to pray to Him. If prayer is the root and praise is the flower, we cannot expect much of a bouquet if the roots are dry and ill-nourished. But when we sink our roots of prayer deeply, we should soon expect brilliant flowers of praise. It is the most natural thing in the world to give God praise when He has overwhelmed us by an answer to our prayer.

PROPHECY OF FUTURE PRAISE

In the second section of Psalm 138 David projects a period of time in which all the kings of the earth will join him in exuberant praise to Yahweh. These are his words:

(4) All the kings of the earth will praise You, O Yahweh,
When they will have heard the words of Your mouth.
(5) And they will sing of the ways of Yahweh.
For great is the glory of Yahweh!
(6) For though Yahweh is exalted He regards the lowly;
But the haughty He knows from afar.

Based on David's adventure in prayer and the surprise of God's response in his own life, the King of Israel now becomes a prophet, directed by the Spirit of God, to predict a future day in which all kings will experience what he has just experienced. Some translations of the Bible suggest that this is merely David's desire, rather than a prophecy. I believe we have here a specific future prophecy of the glorious age of the Messiah. This point of view is reflected in the translation above.

We delight in every example in history of a national leader who has acknowledged the God of Israel and the Father of our Lord Jesus Christ to be his God. Yet we recognize that such praise comes rarely from world leaders. Yet David, led by the Spirit, longs for and projects just such an age. In this time "all the kings of the earth" will join in praise to the glory of Yahweh.

If these words are to be taken seriously, and not just as an exuberant embellishment on the part of David, they must portend the Messianic Age. When King Jesus is ruling on the throne of David (see Is. 9:7), kingship will truly have a new pattern. Unlike those kings who have oppressed the poor to court the nobility, King Jesus' rule will be unique in all human history. As Isaiah describes this reign,

> For He will delight in the fear of Yahweh,
> And not by the seeing of His eyes will He judge,
> Nor by the hearing of His ears will He adjudicate;
> But He will judge in righteousness the poor,
> And He will adjudicate in uprightness the afflicted of the earth;
> And He will strike the earth with the rod of His mouth,
> And by the breath of His lips He will slay the wicked (Is. 11:3,4).

This will be the time when the knowledge of Yahweh will fill the earth as the waters flood the ocean beds (see Is. 11:9). And in that day, Isaiah sings:

> Many people will come and say,
> "Come, let us ascend to the mount of Yahweh,
> To the house of the God of Jacob;
> In order that He may teach us His ways,
> And that we may walk in His paths!"
> For from Zion will instruction proceed,
> And the word of Yahweh from Jerusalem! (Is. 2:3).

With Jesus on His glorious throne, all national leaders under Him will be learning His ways and walking in His paths. As in the case of David (as one before the time), they shall hear His words and join their ancient counterpart in giving public acknowledgment to His name. Hearing of His paths, they will delight in them and sing of them. Hence, our Psalm has these words:

> All the kings of the earth will acknowledge You, O Yahweh,
> When they will have heard the words of Your mouth.
> And they will sing of the ways of Yahweh (Ps. 138:4,5a).

It is in the second colon of verse 5 that we have the central shout or the basic teaching of this Psalm. Psalm 138 is a declarative Psalm of praise by an individual. In this type of Psalm there is one central sentence in which God is lauded or acknowledged. The central sentence of this Psalm—the very heart of the poem—is verse 5b:

> For great is the glory of Yahweh!

From this basic assertion we draw the theme of our Psalm. The great glory of God is demonstrated in this Psalm by His magnificent, overwhelming answer to David's prayer. From this we may extrapolate the principle: *The purpose of prayer is to glorify God.* If David's prayer adventure led him to predict a glorious future when all kings will experience what he had experienced, then *we ought to join now* in the same adventure of prayer. David's experience may be ours. As we pray and as God answers, His glory may be felt in ever-new ways. He may teach of His glory in a manner that will overwhelm us.

After the heart of the Psalm is given in verse 5b, David the king and prophet then utters a proverbial saying. He was also among the wise of ancient Israel:

> For though Yahweh is exalted, yet the lowly He regards,
> But the haughty He knows only from a distance (v. 6).

This verse is one of characteristic paradox in wisdom and hymnic texts. God's glory is limitless, but He stoops to the humble. Those who elevate themselves might think that they would be nearer to God. But their self-aggrandizing glory is relative; His glory is infinite. The proud are distant from the truly exalted Yahweh.

> For thus says the high and exalted One,
> Who dwells forever, whose Name is Holy,
> > "On a high and holy place I dwell,
> > And with the contrite and lowly of spirit;
> > In order to revive the spirit of the lowly,
> > And to revive the heart of the contrite" (Is. 57:15).

PERSPECTIVE FOR A CONTINUED WALK

In the third movement (vv. 7,8), David turns back from his future prediction to a new perspective on his own life in continuing prayerful dependence on God.

> (7) Even though I shall walk in the midst of trouble,
> > You will revive me;
> > Against the wrath of my enemies
> > You will stretch forth Your hand,
> > And Your right hand will save me.
> (8) Yahweh will accomplish that which concerns me;
> > O Yahweh, Your loyal love is everlasting!
> > Do not forsake the works of Your hands!

Even though David has had the dramatic answer to prayer that occasioned this Psalm, and despite the fact that he was graced by the Spirit to set forth the future glorious Messianic Age, he still has a life to live in a tough and unrelenting world. The fact that it is a life of faith makes this life possible (with praise). Just because God has answered one of our prayers in an extraordinary manner does not mean that all of our prayer concerns are behind us. David says that there will be times again when he will be in the "belly of distress."

But because of the dramatic answer to his prayer, the poet who gave us this Scripture states that he has a renewed sense of confidence in God. Each time a prayer is answered, we are encouraged anew to keep on praying. David describes God's acts on his behalf in terms of hand-to-hand combat. The hand of God, even His strong right hand, will lash out against the hot fury of all one's foes.

In words that are almost prescient of Romans 8:28, David displays a new confidence in God's determination to bless him in all respects in His own way. Verse 8a, "Yahweh will accomplish what concerns me," is the Old Testament expression of the New Testament faith: "And we know that God causes all things to work together for good to those who love God, to those who are called according to His purpose" (Rom. 8:28 NASB).

In the last two elements of verse 8, David expresses a significant balance of his theological persuasion and his ongoing dependence on God's goodness. On the one hand, he shouts with confidence, "O Yahweh, Your loyal love is everlasting!" (v. 8b). Here he declares the most central affirmation of the Book of Psalms concerning the character of God. But on the other hand, he prays in exquisite ambivalence that God will not forsake the works of His hands (v. 8c).

Believing in God, he still must pray to God. And so it is with us! The more we affirm the greatness of God, the more we shall increase in our true dependence upon Him. *When we pray we glorify God.*

WITHIN FIVE MINUTES

In December 1974 our family faced a most difficult period of separation, but in our experience we learned something of what David had learned. I was scheduled to lead a seminary tour of the Holy Land. This time my happiness at the prospect of being in Israel was tempered by the realization that our third child was due about the time of my expected return.

One of our group made a telephone call home from Israel early in our trip. This prompted me to think that I should do the same to encourage my wife (and myself) in this time apart from each other. I began to pray that God would lead me to make this call at the very best possible time.

One day I had an overwhelming compulsion that this was the day to place the telephone call. All that day we were visiting Philistine archaeological sites—no chance to make a call there!

After dinner that night I asked the woman at the hotel desk to make a call for me. As this was the end of the Hebrew Sabbath, she warned me that the lines would likely be full and that I would be fortunate to get my call placed in four hours. As a matter of fact, the call was completed by the time I got to my room to wait.

My mother was on the telephone first. I knew she would be surprised, but her weeping of happy tears was more than I had expected. Finally, my wife came on the phone. Her happy tears were even more plentiful than those of my mother.

Then she got out the story. My call from Israel was placed at 8:20 Saturday evening, but it was 10:20 in the morning of the same day in Oregon. Earlier that morning, Beverly had gone into hard labor. She had been on the phone much of the morning implementing "Plan B."

My call came within five minutes of her leaving for the hospital. Our baby boy, Bruce, was born just three hours later. What an answer to prayer for the placing of a telephone call! Never in our marriage had we ever seemed so close together—and so close to God. When God has answered prayer in such an extraordinary manner as this, we cannot help but give praise to His name.

Men ought always to pray. And the purpose of prayer is to glorify God. When God has so honored His name in an answer to prayer, glory must be given to Him.

CHAPTER 12

Psalm 142
A Shriek or a Prayer?

When our need is at its greatest,
The Lord God stretches toward us His hand!
                                        —E. Humperdinck

There are times when it seems that only a shriek or a gasp
will do. Every fall one of America's little heroes lets go with a
desperate shriek. This hero's name is Charlie Brown. Every
October, when the American football season is well underway, Charlie decides he is ready to try to kick a football,
which Lucy promises to hold for him. Year after year Lucy
has pulled the ball out from under him, and poor Charlie has
fallen heavily on his back. But hope springs eternal—at least
in the color comics on Sunday mornings. At this time each
year, he thinks he will make it.

So we watch him again in his annual fall ritual of despera-
tion. Lucy swears by all her gods that this time, this year, she
will play fair. Charlie is excited. "At last," he thinks, "at
last!" He backs up, sights the ball, and begins to run. His little
legs go as fast as they can carry him. Just as he approaches
the ball he kicks with all of his might. But he kicks at the air:
Lucy has done it again. Just as he begins his kick, Lucy pulls
the ball away.

The momentum of the swing of his little leg throws Charlie
off balance. He is thrown up into the air, and he is going to fall
down hard. And on the way down, he does the only thing he
can do. *He shrieks.* The Charlie Brown shriek usually takes

an entire panel of the Charles Schulz cartoon strip. On the way down he shouts, "Aughh!"

There are times in life, when one is on the way down, when such a shriek seems to be the only possible response. As we watch Charlie fall, we laugh—glad that we are not in his britches. We also wait each year for Lucy's new excuse for her perfidy. Her variations on this deviltry seem boundless.

Whenever I read the opening words of Psalm 142 I think of Charlie Brown on the way down. This Psalm evokes that same sense of helplessness. As we shall see, David feels as helpless as Charlie with his legs askew and the cold ground coming up quickly. But the difference is that David's shriek is not a random, meaningless expression, but a purposeful scream to the living God.

In order to demonstrate the validity of the comparison— and contrast—of Charlie Brown and David, we shall have to gain an appreciation for the background of this Psalm by the use of its very helpful superscription.

THE IMPORTANT LITTLE WORDS

There has been an unfortunate tendency in some of the more recent translations of the Bible to depreciate the significance of the superscriptions to the Psalms. The reader of the *Good News Bible in Today's English Version* (TEV), for example, will only find the superscription to this Psalm if he is diligent enough to scan the footnotes. Many critical scholars have long ceased to concern themselves with these notations.[1] We will proceed not only with the conviction that

[1] Barth admits some value to the superscriptions as a late Jewish commentary on the Psalms, but finds no value in them for questions of authorship. See *Introduction,* pp. 6–8. Arguments for the integrity of the superscriptions are given by Gleason L. Archer, Sr., *A Survey of Old Testament Introduction,* rev. ed. (Chicago: Moody, 1974), pp. 443–45. Archer bases his views in part on the rare and difficult terminology as indicators of antiquity. Kidner, *Psalms,* vol. 1, pp. 44, 46, also presents the issue squarely: "What matters is their truth."

the historical notes in the superscriptions are true, but that they are also important. In fact, our appreciation of this Psalm will depend on a study of these words.

Psalm 142 is one of fourteen Psalms that has a specific notice about David's career in relationship to the poem.[2] The superscription for this Psalm reads: "A *maskil* of David, while he was in the cave; a prayer."

The word *maskil* is sufficiently puzzling to be transliterated rather than translated in some editions of the Bible. The word continues to be debated, but it likely means "contemplative poem" or "didactic poem."[3] This Psalm fits such a role nicely, for Psalm 142 gives instruction by example on the nature of successful prayer. We should not force the word *maskil* to the point of implying a "how-to-do-it," but the word does suggest the root meanings of *skill* and *wisdom*. By meditating on this poem we ought to gain skill and wisdom in its principal subject—*prayer.*

The biographical element in this superscription speaks of David's being *in the cave.* Psalm 57 has a similar note from the career of David: "When he fled from Saul, in the cave." These two Psalms (57 and 142) invite comparative study. A concordance survey suggests that the word "cave" in the Old Testament is used with the specific definite article rather than with the generic article. In English one may say, "He has gone to the hospital," but not necessarily be designating a specific hospital by the (generic) article "the." At other times we use "the" in a specific way, when we mean one item and not another. The reference in our Psalm is to a specific cave in which David sought refuge during the struggle that led to this poem.

Twice in the historical narrative of the career of David we learn that he sought refuge in a cave. One was in the cave

[2]The others are Pss. 3,7,18,30,34,51,52,54,56,57,59,60 and 63.

[3]This is one of those terms that argues for the antiquity of these notes. *Maskil* is found in the superscriptions of Pss. 32,42,44,45,52,53,54,55, 74,78,88,89 and 142.

district called Adullam, west of Jerusalem (see 1 Sam. 22:1). The other was one of the caves at En-gedi on the western shore of the Dead Sea (1 Sam. 24:1). Both of these cave incidents were in David's flight from Saul. A reading of Psalm 142 seems to demand the former scene (Adullam) as the setting for the distress that fills this poem.

STEPS TO THE CAVE

To approach our Psalm more fully we need to sketch the incidents that led to David's experience in this cave. First Samuel 20 describes the touching scene of David's final break with Jonathan, a necessary concomitant of Saul's rage against David as his potential rival. This parting of these closest of friends marked David for the rest of his life. Later, on hearing the dreaded news of Jonathan's death on Mount Gilboa, David composed one of his finest Psalms, in which he intoned:

"I am distressed for you, my brother Jonathan;
You have been very pleasant to me.
Your love to me was more wonderful
Than the love of women.
   How have the mighty fallen,
   And the weapons of war perished!" (2 Sam. 1:26,27
NASB).

Cut off from his friend, and an enemy of his king, David fled to the sanctuary for help. When he came to the village of Nob, slightly north of Jerusalem, David was met by a trembling high priest, Ahimelech (1 Sam. 21:1). David was fed with the bread of the Presence and armed with the sword of Goliath, the giant of Gath whom David had defeated on a happier day (see 1 Sam. 17). Bread that was not to be eaten and a sword too large to use—such was the help he got that day. Further, an agent of Saul observed these bizarre activities. This spy, Doeg the Edomite, exposed the priests to Saul, who then killed them, their families, and even their animals in a grotesque massacre (see 1 Sam. 22:9–19).

David, in despair and flight, made his way to the city of his former foe—to Gath, the home city of Goliath! At first he was welcomed by Achish, the king of the city. But then some of the king's advisors began to suspect some chicanery on the part of their unlikely guest. David escaped with his life only by feigning madness, drooling in his beard, muttering senselessly, and writing graffiti on the city gate. Achish let him go, declaring he had sufficient madmen of his own; he did not need to import one (see 1 Sam. 21:10–15).

NO FRIENDS IN THE CAVE

Then David came to the cave! (see 1 Sam. 22:1). His relatives came to him there, and so did those who were in distress, in debt, or discontent (v. 2). Four hundred men joined him, but their presence was little comfort. Most were there not because of an allegiance to him. Rather, they were there as outcasts, misfits, enemies of the state, and adventurers.

David looked about him in the cave and realized what a mockery his condition was to the promise given him in his anointing by Samuel (see 1 Sam. 16:13). Promised by God's man to become king of the nation, he finds himself as a fugitive captain in a cave filled with kooks.

Then he shrieks! Like Charlie Brown on the way down, David then screams aloud. But his scream is like Charlie's only in its intensity and feeling of helplessness; the content is different. While Charlie can only shout an *aughh* of helplessness, David screams to the God of all care, though he teeters on the brink of despair.

We could have jumped right into a discussion of the Psalm, but it seems that this historical setting is necessary if the deep emotion of the Psalm is to be understood.

Psalm 142 presents a *maskil* on prayer, a lesson on the

nature of praying successfully. The message of the Psalm is basic to a theology of prayer: *Successful prayer is based on an unqualified dependence on the mercy of Yahweh.*

A SINCERE INTENSITY

The first strophe of this didactic Psalm stresses that *successful prayer is expressed in a sincere intensity.* Listen to these words of David as he shrieks "on the way down":

(1) Aloud to Yahweh I scream out;
     Aloud to Yahweh I implore favor!
(2) I pour out before Him my trouble;
     My distress before Him I make known.

This Psalm is another example of the Psalms of the lament of the individual. Considering the brevity of the Psalm, the opening words (vv. 1,2) present an unusually strong introductory cry for help. The four members of these two verses show a tremendous intensity of expression.[4]

In these words there is an expression of grief, but done in prayer. These words suggest elements often lacking in our own prayers. Prayer is many things, of course. By prayer we talk to our Lord; by prayer we commune with Him. In private prayer we may render thanksgiving to Him and in public prayer we may offer God our praise.

But basically *prayer is asking.* So often are we encouraged to balance our prayer life with expressions other than *just* asking, we may forget what prayer basically is meant to be. All the Hebrew and Greek words for prayer are words for *asking.* In prayer we are to show our dependence, our *unqualified dependence,* on the mercy of God.

[4]In the original text verse 1 has synonymous parallelism of the members, with the parallel words in the same order. In verse 2 there is synonymous parallelism as well, but the parallel words are in reverse order (chiasm).

How often our own prayer seems to be deficient in the *intensity* we find in this Psalm! A pastor friend once began the pastoral prayer for the congregation one Sunday morning in these words: "Our Father, we thank You for this food." Then he caught himself, realized what he had said, where he was, and paused awkwardly, wondering how to recover. He lamely continued, ". . . this food, uh . . . , which we are about to receive from Your word."

Sometimes our prayers seem to be just as careless and thoughtless. Perhaps this is one reason why God allows a measure of distress to come into our lives from time to time, so that we may learn anew to express our needs in earnest and in intensity.

The intensity of David's prayer is demonstrated in the verbs "I scream out," "I implore favor," "I pour out," and "I make known." These verbs are further emphasized by the adverbial forms of verse 1, "aloud" (given twice). David was not mumbling in his beard to God; he was praying in earnest, for life was at stake.

ON TROUBLING VIRTUES

But intensity, like sincerity, is not sufficient by itself to please God. There are countless pagans who are both intense and sincere, but whose prayers are futile, a chasing after wind (see Eccl. 1:14).

Dr. Charles Ryrie once published a gospel tract illustrating the futility of sincerity apart from truth. On the front of the tract was a *Peanuts* cartoon strip (many theologians read Schulz!), and Charlie was being berated by Lucy for yet another embarrassing baseball loss. Charlie's excuse was that at least he was sincere. Sincerity is commendable, but *by itself* it does not win games—nor please God. It is possible to be sincere—and wrong.

Those four hundred fifty prophets of Baal who prayed to

their imagined deity were both sincere and intense in their calls for fire to ignite their altar in their classic confrontation with Elijah (see 1 Kin. 18). With no answer from their god, and with Elijah's biting sarcasm and ribald scorn goading them to renewed efforts, "They cried with a loud voice and cut themselves according to their custom with swords and lances until the blood gushed out on them" (1 Kin. 18:28 NASB).

Now that is intensity! But despite their frantic acts that lasted almost the entire day, their sincerity and intensity were rewarded grimly. For, "There was no voice, no one answered, and no one paid attention" (v. 29 NASB).

Sincerity and intensity are troubling virtues. It is impossible to please God without being both sincere and intense in one's relationship to Him. The basic creed of Israel in the Torah stresses love for God with all of one's being (see Deut. 6:4–10). Regularly the prophets speak God's harsh words of condemnation on all acts of piety done with less than a right heart attitude toward Him (see Is. 1:10–15). Yet *mere* sincerity and intensity will not please Him either, if wrongly directed.

The true sincerity and intensity of David in our Psalm are expressed in direct address to the living Yahweh. In the four cola of verses 1 to 2, there are four references to the Lord as the one addressed in prayer ("to Yahweh," twice in verse 1, and "before Him," twice in verse 2).

David's use of the name of God, Yahweh, in prayer is the Old Testament equivalent of our prayers addressed "in Jesus' name." When we add these words to our prayers, we are not to think of them as a mere liturgical phrase, a spiritual hiccup to keep our prayers kosher. It is by these words that we affirm that the only right we have to pray is based on our relationship to the risen Christ who is our priest in the presence of the Father (see Heb. 4:14–16; 7:24, 25; 8:1,2; cf. John 14:13,14; 15:16; 16:23–28). When David prays "to Yahweh," he is praying not only with intensity, he is praying rightly.

Besides being intense and in direct address to the Lord of

reality, David's prayer is also specific. We have all heard messages on prayer in which preachers have stressed the element of specificity. Yet at times we still pray with our random shots: "Bless all the missionaries!" In David's Psalm on prayer we find a strong level of specificity in the words "my trouble" and "my distress" (v. 2). These words grow out of the turmoil in his life as we have already surveyed. David expressed to God the nature of his trouble and the particulars of his distress.

Many of the model prayers in the Bible, from that of Daniel (see Dan. 9:3–19) to that of Jesus (see John 17:1–26), have these three characteristics we have found in David's prayer in Psalm 142:1,2: intensity, specificity, and direct address toward God—based on a personal relationship with Him.

MANIFEST HELPLESSNESS

The second movement of Psalm 142 expresses *a manifest sense of helplessness*. These are David's words of lament:

(3) When my spirit was overwhelmed within me—
     But You, You know my path!—
   In any way I might walk
   They have set a trap for me.
(4) Look to my right hand and see!
     There is no one who pays attention to me.
   Escape has perished from me,
     No one cares for my life.

Sometimes periods of such dejection and despair may come that it seems that there is no out, no escape, and no help. Such feelings may come in childhood with a minor, but deeply felt frustration; they may also come in maturity with pain increased by the accumulation of one's years.

One afternoon I observed a three-year-old boy looking for

his older brother. The older brother had awakened first from a nap and had gone out of the house. When the younger brother awakened, he saw that his brother was not in the next bed. Wordlessly, he made his way around the house, searching for his brother. As his mother followed his progress through the house, she observed that he did not say anything; he just kept looking. Finally, he made his way to the bathroom, slumped in a far corner against the wall, shook his head, and said over and over, "My brother is nowhere; my brother is nowhere." The pain of his frustration marked his being.

By now the pronouns of a lament in Hebrew psalmody are familiar to you. David complains using the three pronouns, "I," "You," and "they." The first person pronoun is used in verse 3a in the words, "my spirit was overwhelmed within me." The Hebrew verb used here is particularly strong and expressive of a sense of helplessness. This form is used by Jonah as he was nearly drowned (see Jon. 2:7a), by Asaph as he was in a sleepless torment (see Ps. 77:3b), by David in an almost deathlike experience (see Ps. 143:4), and in Psalm 107 of a caravan lost in the desert (Ps. 107:5). It is a word aptly chosen to express his helplessness and frustration as David cowered in the cave.

NO EXIT

The pronoun "they" is used in these Psalms of lament to express the machinations of the enemy as the believer feels pressure from the outside. The cave district of Adullam is quite extensive. By clever maneuvers, David and his gang of cut-throats might have eluded Saul's soldiers for some time by working their way through various tunnels from one cave to another. This region was later to host Jewish refugees from Roman soldiers, and even later Christians under persecution.

But while there was a relative measure of safety within the

cave area, there was still *no escape*. Jean-Paul Sartre once wrote a terrifying play in which he described hell as a room from which there was "no exit." In David's case, Saul's army would have surrounded the region and blocked off all exits. David's distress is given in these words:

> In any way I might walk
> They have set a trap for me (v. 3cd).

Whatever route he might decide upon would lead him to the traps of his pursuers. The word "trap" in the original text is regularly used for a figurative expression of calamity and plotting (for examples, see Pss. 91:3; 124:7; 140:5). It is specifically the term for a bird trap, which brings sudden destruction to fowl.

A WORD OF TRUST

In verse 3 we have seen the "I" and the "they" elements of the lament. The middle colon of this verse seems to be out of place: "But You, You know my path!" Aside from the wordplay ("path" and "way") in this verse, it is most surprising to find the confession of trust in the middle of the lament! But that is precisely the case in this Psalm. Moreover, the wording of the brief confession is striking. The words "but You" form the *"waw* adversative" as we found in Psalm 13:5 ("but I").[5] Yet normally this *waw* adversative comes at a point of transition in a Psalm, the shifting from petition to praise. Here it is not in a transition at all, but *right in the lament.*

When we have established the general patterns in the Psalms and then come across variations from those patterns, it is likely that a reason for the variations may be found within the demands of the given Psalm. In Psalm 142 the

[5]See Chapter 10.

"You" element of the lament is so very strong (v. 4a, see below) that the poet must anticipate a charge of borderline heresy by an early confession of his trust in God.

For this reason, David's strong—and unexpected—words of trust (though in the bowels of despair) state that ultimately God does know the way out for him. The spiritual stratification of these Psalms of lament seems to interplay between a bedrock of trust and a sheet of doubt.

NO SHIELD

This leads us then to the "You" element of the lament in verse 4. Here are the words again:

Look to my right hand and see!
    There is no one who pays attention to me.
    Escape has perished from me,
    No one cares for my life.

Only some of the more recent English translations of the Bible have dared to translate this verse literally. There is an ancient tradition that we find in the Septuagint that has softened the attack on God in this verse in this way: *"I looked* on my right hand and *beheld . . ."* (KJV, also TEV and many others).

The original text, however, is best understood with reference to God: "(You) look!" That is, David accuses God of not paying attention to his needs. No one cares for him, and it seems not even God is concerned.

The image that David seems to be using is that of a shield. In the ancient Near East one man's shield held in his left hand would protect his own left side and his neighbor's right hand. David already had confessed Yahweh to be his shield (Ps. 3:3). Now, however, he claims to be defenseless. There is no one on his right hand. Even God's shield seems to be removed! Thus his shriek: "Look! See! There is no one!"

As David gropes about the dimness of his cave he finds men there who have come for their own benefit. None is there for David's good; no one cares for his life distress; hence, all escape has perished from him.

In all of this experience, David has presented a picture of helplessness. What we extract from his experience is that successful prayer is motivated by *a manifest sense of helplessness*. There is one more necessary element, which we find in the next verses.

ONGOING DEPENDENCE

In addition to the sincere intensity of the first verses and the manifest helplessness in the next verses, the third section suggests that successful prayer is girded by an *ongoing dependence* on Yahweh's mercy (vv. 5–7). These verses may be read:

(5) I scream out to You, O Yahweh;
I say, "You are my refuge,
My portion in the land of the living!"

(6) Pay attention to my ringing cry,
For I am exceedingly low;
Deliver me from my persecutors,
For they are stronger than I.

(7) Bring me out of this prison,
So that I may give public acknowledgment to Your name.
The righteous will encrown me,
For You will have done bountifully with me.

Several elements of the lament Psalms all come together in this section of the poem. That which holds these verses together as a unit is the sense of ongoing dependence on God on the part of David. In his lament against God, David has almost gone the limit in charging God with not caring (v. 4a).

But on reflection he realizes that if indeed God does *not* care, then he is most hopeless indeed. He *has* to cry out to God; there is none else to whom he may turn. As Peter would say to our Lord when asked if he would leave Him: "Lord, to whom shall we go? You have words of eternal life" (John 6:68 NASB).

His confession of trust, which began prematurely in verse 3b, is now given in strong voice in verse 5. David cries out to Yahweh using the same verb "cry" or "scream" that we found in verse 1a. In this cry he declares God to be his only refuge and portion.

With Saul's army outside, and an unpredictable lot within, David's only hope is to keep on trusting God. David is to keep on being dependent, *even* when he has doubts about that course of action. This is because *there is no other alternative.* If God has abandoned one of His own, then there is absolutely no hope for that person. This means that even if we begin to feel that God no longer cares, we *must* keep on trusting, for we have none but Him. Beneath the vein of doubt, there must be the bedrock of faith. Further, the expression of the third colon of verse 3, "my portion in the land of the living," seems most appropriate and instructive. It is not just that God is our only hope for heaven; He is our only hope now as well!

Verse 6 presents the petitions interspersed with motivations for God to respond to the psalmist. In this Psalm there are the two common verbs of petition, "Hear!" and "Save!" that we have seen in earlier studies.[6] There is no verb "Punish!" in Psalm 142. The verb "to save" is doubled. David shouts:

> Pay attention to my ringing cry! (v. 6a, "Hear!")
> Deliver me from my persecutors! (v. 6c, "Save!")
> Bring me out of this prison! (v. 7a, "Save!")

The same intensity that marked the opening words of this

[6]Again, see the treatment of Psalm 6 in Chapter 3 and that of Psalm 13 in Chapter 10.

Psalm may be seen in these strong verbs of petition. The motivations that David gives are in alternating sequence with the verbs of petition:

> For I am exceedingly low (v. 6b);
> For they are stronger than I (v. 6d).

Here again we have what the Psalm is about: *Successful prayer is based on an unqualified dependence on the mercy of God.* When I find myself in a helpless situation, I affirm only God is my help. When I find myself in a hopeless strait, I declare only God is my hope. When all else fails, He is still sure. When there is no one else, He is still able. In these moments of great despair, we find that our God is still there.

WHEN ALL ELSE FAILS

A television series that was popular several years ago was entitled *Run for Your Life!* The premise of the program concerned a virile young man who found himself living under the specter of imminent death because of a rare and untreatable disease. The knowledge of this led the protagonist to quit his job and "run for his life" in many adventures, wandering the world over as a modern Odysseus.

One adventure had him a captive in a totalitarian state, undergoing brutal brainwashing. Level after level of his memory and consciousness was stripped away. He did everything he could to maintain his sanity. He recited familiar facts, worked through the multiplication tables, and mumbled anything he could to show that he still had some grasp of reality. But each level was stripped away by his tormentors.

Then came one scene that is etched in my memory. The camera looked down into his padded cell. The hero was sprawled on the floor, quietly singing. His song was most surprising for an adventure program on U.S. commercial TV:

Jesus loves me,
This I know,
For the Bible tells me so!

Presumably this song had been taught to him as a young lad. When all else was gone, this one song remained his last grasp on reality. In the end he called on the Savior of the Scriptures.

Similarly David in the melancholy of his cave, with all other defenses gone, must claim again his only sure defense, the Savior of the Scriptures. We are not to suppose that the *only* time one needs to turn to God is when all else has failed. But there are times in life when all else *has* failed, and we realize anew how much we really do need to depend on Him. It is this *ongoing sense of dependence on God's mercy* that Psalm 142 displays.

A CROWN OF PEOPLE

In verse 7b David gives his vow of praise—a distinctive of this type of Psalm. *In distress* he trusts God for release; *in release* he promises to praise God for his deliverance. He asks God to bring him out from his prison-like box in order that he might be able to give public acknowledgment to the name of God. Here we see again what many Psalms display: Praise is public and vocal and comes as a response to the person and actions of God. David longs for a day in which he will be able to praise God in the presence of the community. Prayer is the rootage, and praise is the flower. We pray for God's aid; we praise Him for who He is and for what He does on our behalf.

Psalm 142 concludes on a lovely note of assurance that God has heard. He will deliver, and He will magnify His great name. David sings:

The righteous will encrown me,
For You will have done bountifully with me! (v. 7cd).

PSALM 142: A SHRIEK OR A PRAYER?

This Psalm that began in a shriek ends in a song. Looking forward to the time of Yahweh's deliverance—an act of faith, David projects the community of the faithful surrounding him in response to his praise to the God of his salvation. These people will become David's crown as they join him in magnifying God for His greatness. Together the community will rejoice that only God could have done what was done, and that He again has done all things well.

Hansel and Gretel is a delightful opera, filled with witches, magic, and a dentist's nightmare in terms of candy. Yet there is an underlying moral of great theological significance in this work. Engelbert Humperdinck closes his opera with these words:

> *Wenn die Not aufs Höchste steight*
> *Gott der Herr die Hand uns reicht.*
> (When our need is at its greatest,
> The Lord God stretches toward us His hand.)

These words in the children's story are as true as God's bright tomorrow, and they are remarkably well suited for the conclusion of our study of Psalm 142. But for God's hand of help we must pray, and we must pray rightly. *Successful prayer is based on an unqualified dependence on the mercy of God.*

CHAPTER 13

Psalm 65
When Creation Sings

Joy to the earth! The Savior reigns!
Let men their songs employ;
While fields and floods, rocks, hills and plains
Repeat the sounding joy.

No more let sins and sorrows grow,
Nor thorns infest the ground;
He comes to make His blessings flow
Far as the curse is found.

—Isaac Watts

Imagine for a moment that you are in a concert hall in a choice seat, beside a welcome companion. The two of you are eagerly awaiting the beginning of a musical evening. There is the customary shuffling of programs and the anxious whispering of other concert goers all around you. The musicians in the pit have completed their mildly cacophonous warming-up exercises, and then they tune to concert pitch. Behind the luxurious curtains you know there is a massed choir ready to sing.

Then the musicians come to attention. The whispering of the audience is replaced by applause as the conductor makes his way to the podium. He bows and receives the generous accolade his audience gives him in trust. He then turns to his orchestra, taps on his music stand, and raises his powerful arms.

The instruments are raised, and silence sweeps through the room as all are in preparation for song. But, alas, the conductor does not give the downbeat! There is *no music*.

This imaginary trip to a concert hall where the promise of music came to naught is no less surprising than Psalm 65, the Psalm that promises a song but which begins in silence.

A VOW TO PRAISE

The superscription to Psalm 65 is as filled with the promise of music as the program notes for our imaginary nonconcert. The heading reads this way: "To the choir director. A Psalm of David. A song."

By three indicators we prepare ourselves for music. This is a piece in the collection of the choir director. It is a Psalm of David. Moreover, it is a song to be sung. But this Psalm begins in the sound of silence. Here is the first, surprising movement:

(1) To You there is silence of praise,
     O God in Zion;
   But to You the vow will be performed.
(2) O hearer of prayer,
     To You all men will come.
(3) As for iniquitous matters,
     They prevail over me!
   Our transgressions You will cover.
(4)   O how happy—
       is the one whom You choose and draw near;
       He will abide in Your courts.
       We shall be sated with the goodness of Your
         house,
       even Your holy temple.

In these splendid words we learn that there is *a vow of praise yet to be performed*. As the Psalm progresses we shall find this fits into the larger message: *In the year of His goodness creation will sing.*

SILENT PRAISE?

Of the many verses studied in this book, the first verse of Psalm 65 is one of the most difficult to translate clearly. The reason for the difficulty lies not in obscure terms, but in an improbable linking of two mutually exclusive words. The original text reads, "to You silence praise" (v. 1a).

In these words we have an incongruous association of "silence" and "praise" that defies all hymnic analogy. Praise in the Psalter involves sound. How then may "silence" and "praise" be used together?

One solution, offered by Delitzsch over a century ago, is that silence may substitute for praise; there is a "praise of pious resignation."[1] This idea is echoed by Kidner, who suggests, "It may sometimes be the height of worship, in other words, to fall silent before God in awe at His presence and in submission to His will."[2] It is difficult to quarrel theologically with the genuine piety of humble submission to God's majesty and glory (à la Delitzsch) or with the sentiment of silent admiration in the presence of God (so Kidner).

Nevertheless, "silent praise" is a phrase like "dry water," "cold fire," or "boiling snow." Praise, to repeat, is *not silent* in Old Testament culture. The Old Testament prophets called for *silence* ("Hush!" as in Hab. 2:20; Zech. 2:13; Zeph. 1:7), not for the praise of God, but for fear before God when He was about to break forth in terrible judgment. The proper response to God's glory is *song*.

Silence is what so troubled Isaiah when he saw King

[1]Delitzsch, *Psalms,* vol. 2, pp. 224–26.
[2]Kidner, *Psalms,* vol. 1, p. 230. The Living Bible seems to follow a similar approach in the words, "O God in Zion, we wait before you in silent praise, and thus fulfill our vow."

Yahweh in His royal palace. Yahweh was surrounded by seraphs who shouted in song the inexpressible holiness of God. On seeing the glory of Yahweh, and in observing the decibel level of the angels' song shaking the very foundations of the building, Isaiah gasps:

> Woe is me, for *I am silenced.*
> For a man of unclean lips am I,
> And in the midst of a people of unclean lips I dwell,
> For the King, Yahweh of Hosts, my eyes have seen (Is. 6:5).

Isaiah's gasp is sometimes rendered "I am ruined" (as in the NASB), but this Hebrew verb seems best translated "I am silenced," as this so nicely fits the prophetic lament about his *lips*. He cannot join the angels in praise of God because of the new reality of his sin. His emphasis on his lips being unclean fits with his desire not to be silent, but to shout to Yahweh's glory.

A SILENCE OF PRAISE

In Psalm 65:1 we find that many English translations of the Bible have attempted to express the incongruous linking of the words "silence" and "praise." It does not seem possible that the Hebrew word "silence" can be the equivalent of praise. Rather it is used to indicate an *anticipation* of praise in the words "waiteth" (KJV, ASV), "is due" (RSV), and "is rightfully yours" (JB). However, in the context of the Psalm as a whole, I suggest there is not only an anticipation of praise, but an antithetical parallelism in the verse as well. For this reason my translation reads:

> To You there is *silence of praise,*
> O God in Zion;
> *But* to You the vow will be performed.

That is, there is a type of praise to God that is not now being heard, but which will one day be accomplished. The fulfillment of the vow is certain.[3] We have come to the concert, but there is no music . . . yet! But there *will* be music, as we shall see at the end of this Psalm.

Psalm 65 has often been described as a harvest Psalm, giving praise to God for a bounteous year. The Psalm may well have been used this way in the worship services of Israel. But it seems far more in keeping with the thrust of this hymn to understand it as a prophetic Psalm of praise. In this Psalm we may see an anticipation of the rule of King Jesus when all creation will be restored to Edenic conditions. The praise that is now "silent" is the bounty of the renovated earth in the reversal of the curse that God has placed on the ground (see Gen. 3:17–19).

LONGING OF CREATION

Psalm 65 is best presented as a hymn of anticipation of a new voice in the praise of God, the unrestrained and unhindered voice of creation to her Creator. This Psalm anticipates Paul's exposition of the theme of future restitution in Romans 8:18–22. His introductory words read as follows:

> For I consider that the sufferings of this present time are not worthy to be compared with the glory that is to be revealed to us. For the anxious longing of the creation waits eagerly for the revealing of the sons of God (Rom. 8:18,19 NASB).

Paul then reveals the intention of God respecting His curse on creation:

[3]The NASB avoids the difficulty of the verse by reading, "There will be silence before Thee, and praise in Zion, O God." In this approach silence and praise join hands—an unlikely event! Dahood's recasting, "Praise to you in the mighty castle" (*Psalms II,* pp. 109–10), seems improbable as well.

For the creation was subjected to futility, not of its own will, but because of Him who subjected it, in hope that the creation itself also will be set free from its slavery to corruption into the freedom of the glory of the children of God. For we know that the whole creation groans and suffers the pains of childbirth together until now (Rom. 8:20–22 NASB).

In Romans 8 Paul describes the present state of creation as a woman in the pain of childbirth. But her pain is *in hope* of release. Our Psalm describes the release in prophetic terms. Just as Isaiah 11 details the effects of the rule of King Jesus on animal behavior, when carnivores will become herbivores and predators will lie down with their prey (see Is. 11:6–8), so Psalm 65 depicts the coming change in agricultural produce when all creation will praise God as it has promised. For this reason our Psalm begins by saying that there is presently a silence of praise to God in Zion. The vow will be performed, for God will lift the curse.

THE RULE OF THE BRANCH

In verses 2 to 4 of Psalm 65 this promise is built upon and expanded in terms of its effects on the godly. The Psalm speaks of creation, but it is more concerned with people. In this factor we find another close similarity in our Psalm to Isaiah 11. In that passage the climax of the description of the changes in animal behavior comes in verse 9:

They will not hurt or destroy in all My holy mountain,
For the earth will be as full of the knowledge of Yahweh
As the waters cover the ocean beds.

The antecedents to the pronouns *they* in this verse are the varied animals of verses 6–8; but the implication is that *people* will know the knowledge of Yahweh. Verse 10 speaks

of an international body of believers coming to the Beautiful
Branch:

> He will stand as a banner for the peoples,
> And His resting place will be glorious (Is. 11:10b).

Verses 11–16 describe the second exodus of Israel "from the
four corners of the earth" (v. 12d). In this new work of God's
deliverance there is an act more stunning than wolves who
dwell with lambs: God's *people* will live in unity as well (v.
13).

So in our text, Psalm 65, the effects of God's rule in the lives
of people are not forgotten. Similar to Isaiah 11:10, there is an
international response to God's grace in verse 2: "O hearer of
prayer, To You all men will come."

The thought of all men coming to Israel's God would cause
many in ancient Israel to ask, "But what of their sin which
separates them from Him?" David responds to this implicit
question with an assertion admitting his own sin: "Iniquitous
matters prevail against me!" (v. 3a). But then he adds that
God in grace will forgive all our rebellions: "As for our transgressions, You will atone for them" (v. 3b).

The emphatic pronoun "You" in this passage reminds the
reader of the great surprise to the sinner that God is his
Savior. Isaiah 12:1 describes a similar delight:

> Then you will say on that day,
>   "I give public acknowledgment to You, O Yahweh;
>   For You were angry with me,
>   But Your anger has turned away;
>   Now You comfort me."

These words have their ultimate setting in the choirs of the
redeemed in the millennial kingdom. The context is that of
the rule of the Beautiful Branch of Isaiah 11. But these words
are also an expression of the gospel for all ages. *God,* against

whom every sin is rebellion and affront, is the One who is *Savior* from all sin (see Is. 12:2).

For this reason born of joy, the psalmist exults in God's blessing to forgiven sinners who may now delight in His presence:

> O how happy is the one whom You choose and draw near,
> He will abide in Your courts.
> We shall be sated with the goodness of Your house,
> Even Your holy temple (Ps. 65:4).

Isaiah's millennial Psalm ends in similar joy:

> Cry in great joy, O citizen of Zion,
> For great in your midst is the Holy One of Israel!
> (Is. 12:6).

The first movement of Psalm 65 presents *a vow of praise yet to be fulfilled*. We are not told in this first strophe what shall be the occasion for the praise that this Psalm promises. Only as we read through the end of the Psalm do we learn the thesis of the Psalm: *In the year of God's goodness creation will sing*. The word "goodness" in verse 4 ties the first strophe to the third, where the words "the year of Your goodness" are prominent (v. 11; see p. 211).

A PRAYER TO OUR KING

The second movement of Psalm 65, verses 5 to 8, emphasizes the fact that *Yahweh is able to answer our yearning prayer*. These verses of the Psalm are words of descriptive praise, introduced and concluded with strong imperatives of prayer.

> (5) By awesome deeds in righteousness answer us,
> O God of our salvation,

> The confidence of all the ends of the earth
> and the distant sea;
> (6) Who established the mountains by His strength,
> Being girded with might;
> (7) Who silences the roaring of the seas,
> The roaring of their waves,
> Even the tumult of the peoples;
> (8) While those who dwell at the ends of the earth
> Stand in awe at Your signs.
> Make dawn and sunset shout for joy!

Our strophe begins with a strong assumption of God's ability to answer our yearning prayer. The words "by awesome deeds" of verse 5a serve to introduce the prayer. Similar words are picked up in the praise section in verse 8a, "those . . . stood in awe." Word plays such as this are a delight to eye and ear, and they help to hold the Psalm together.

The psalmist's appeal to God's "awesome deeds" is coupled to Yahweh's matchless character, as he adds "in righteousness." Our God may indeed act in ways that fill all with awe, but He can never act against the excellencies of His character. This is in part why the psalmists regularly praise God for being good. Psalm 106:1,2, for example, ties together the goodness of God and His mighty deeds.

We may never exhaust our praise for the mighty or awesome deeds of our Lord. The reason we wish to praise Him is that His acts conform to His character. They are awesome, but in righteousness; they are mighty, but they proceed from His goodness and His loyal love.

The middle part of the second movement of Psalm 65 has some mystery to it. Some of the terminology is borrowed from the mythological expressions of Canaanite religion. The exclusive monotheism of the Old Testament faith never condones polytheism, but the poets of the Bible often used terminology from Canaanite poets in a figurative way to praise God and to despoil paganism at the same time. The words used in this section praise God as Creator against the backdrop of the Canaanite myth of titanic struggles between deities of chaos (the sea and its lackeys) and cosmos (Baal, the young champion god of fertility).[4]

In these words of praise we affirm Yahweh as the One who has established mountains and silenced seas. He is the one who has made subject all creatures everywhere. The expressions, "the ends of the earth, and the distant sea" (v. 5cd; cf. v. 8a), show the universalism of the Old Testament faith already given in verse 2b to be made most prominent. God, who has created all of the universe, will subject the earth to His name.

The words of the second part of verse 5 are in perfect accord with the intent of God's will expressed at the very beginning of His exclusive choice of Abraham. The seventh element of the Abrahamic blessing demonstrates the universal extent of God's saving grace: "And in you all the families of the earth shall be blessed" (Gen. 12:3c).

IN PRAISE OF THE KING

By virtue of creation God is King over all the earth (see Ps. 93:1,2). As Savior He is King over all His people (see Ps. 47:6). As the Coming One, He will reign over all nations as their King (see Ps. 47:9). These three aspects of the rule of King Yahweh are regularly interplayed by the poets of the Old Testament. He *is* King, for He has created all; He *becomes* King, as He is received as Savior; He *will be* King, as He comes to rule on the throne of David (see Is. 9:7).

All three aspects are found in our Psalm. God is the Creator (vv. 6,7), He is our Savior (v. 5), and He is the Coming One (v. 9, see p. 210). The truths that He is the Creator of all and the Savior of His people give assurance that *God is able to answer*

[4]Bruce K. Waltke deals with these issues in his lectures entitled *Creation and Chaos* (Portland: Western Baptist Seminary, 1974).

our yearning prayer. When we have such stirring words evoking the image of the majesty of our King, then we are compelled to trust, to praise, and to pray.

This strophe ends as it begins with strong words of prayer. Verse 8b reads, "Make dawn and sunset shout for joy!"[5] These words call to mind Yahweh's challenge to Job from the whirlwind as He asserts His sovereign mystery as the solitary Creator of all that is. Of that creation, God asks Job where he was when God laid the foundations of the earth (Job 38:4a). Then He adds:

> When the morning stars sang together,
> And all the sons of God shouted for joy? (v. 7).

It seems that David is calling for God *to renew the song.* As the morning stars joined the angels in praising God in the original creation, so David prays (and we join with him) that God will cause creation to sing anew. The words "dawn and sunset" refer to the totality of the earth. This is a poetic device (merism) where opposites are used to express totality. All of the earth is to praise God, her Creator King.

God is praised for being the One who is able to answer this prayer. This prayer is an Old Testament poetic way of saying, "Amen, Come, Lord Jesus" (Rev. 22:20). To the King of creation, who is also the King our Savior, comes the prayer to institute His reign over a reconstituted earth.

A VISIT OF THE KING

In this third section of the poem we find that *in visiting the earth Yahweh will institute the year of His goodness* (vv. 9–13). The verbs in the following translation are taken as prophetic perfects (and are translated as futures). Verses 9 to

---

[5]I take the Hebrew imperfects in verse 5 ("answer") and verse 8 ("make shout") as having imperatival force; cf. Dahood, *Psalms II,* pp. 108, 111, 113.

13 depict in a highly emotive way the fulfillment of the vow of verses 1 to 4 and the answer to the prayer of verses 5 to 8.

(9) You will visit the earth and make it abundant;
    You will greatly enrich it;
    The channel of God will be full of water;
    You will provide her grain,
    For this You established her.

(10) You will drench her furrows;
    You will soak down her ridges;
    You will soften her with copious showers;
    You will bless its growth.

(11) You will crown the year of Your goodness,
    Your wagon tracks will trickle luxuriance.

(12) The pastures of the wilderness will trickle
    And the hills will gird themselves with rejoicing.

(13) The meadows will be dressed in flocks,
    And the valleys will be enveloped with grain;
        They will shout for joy,
        Yes, they will sing!

In this passage the key verb is "to visit." The Hebrew word translated "to visit" is used often in the Old Testament, with a wide range of meaning. The word develops from the idea of "to miss," through that of "to observe with care," to that of "to visit."

Yahweh the Ever-Present (see Ps. 139:7–12) is said "to visit" His people in special acts of grace and provision (see Gen. 21:1; Ruth 1:6). He also "visits" the wicked in strong acts of retribution and punishment (see Jer. 6:15; Ps. 59:5). The context of this Psalm leaves no doubt that this "visit" of God is all of grace.

As noted before, many have taken our Psalm to be a harvest poem. But to describe every rainfall as a "visit" from Yahweh seems too close to Baalism to be the intent of this verb in our text. Baal was believed to be the god of rain and fertility in the Canaanite system. The lightning was the casting of his spear; thunder was the beating of his heavenly drums; the clouds were his chariot as he brought rain to the land.[6]

The prophetic perspective suggested in this study allows for the Hebrew verb "to visit" to be used in a most significant manner: Yahweh the great King is (soon) to visit His earth and to restore its intended abundance.

THE CHANNEL OF GOD

The words of verses 9 and 10 describe in fine hyperbole the plenteous water God will bring to a thirsty land. This is a regular image of prophecies of the coming kingdom age. In one of his splendid descriptions of the coming rule of King Jesus, Isaiah couples plenteous water with the fulness of the Spirit:

> For I will pour out water on the thirsty land;
> And torrents will flow on the dry land;
> I will pour out My Spirit on your seed,
> Even My blessing on your descendants (Is. 44:3).

In verses 9 and 10 of our Psalm the water comes so generously and graciously that we are caused to enjoy it almost as a cabbage might. C. S. Lewis speaks of the "feel" of weather in these words:

> What they do give us, far more sensuously and delightedly than anything I have seen in Greek, is the very feel of weather—weather seen with a real countryman's eyes, enjoyed almost as a vegetable might be supposed to enjoy it.[7]

---

[6]These issues relate directly to the story of Elijah in his confrontation with the prophets of Baal on Mount Carmel; cf. my paper "Elijah the Broken Prophet," *Journal of the Evangelical Theological Society*, XXII (Sept., 1979).

[7]Lewis, *Reflections*, p. 77. He cites as well Psalm 104:16a, "The trees of Yahweh drink their fill."

What a contrast this poem presents to the uncertainties of weather that farmers the world over regularly face today. Now flooding, now drought; now too early, now too late; this year sufficient, next year a guess—the alternation of the unexpected becomes the expected when we think of rain in terms of world agricultural needs. Those Israeli farmers in the wilderness of Judah who plant winter wheat each year, only to harvest one year in five, long for a generous supply of rainfall. Those Filipino farmers in the provinces of Luzon who find their rice paddies flooded and their harvests destroyed because of monsoon rains, long for a helpful supply of rainfall.

The story is as old as famine in Old Testament Egypt and Canaan: Good years are interspersed with the bad; rain comes in blessed sufficiency or in sporadic devastation. But one day God the Creator King will *visit* this earth and make it gloriously abundant. One day the "river of God" will be full, and rain will come in gracious provision as God actively blesses the growth of the earth. This is what He has made the earth to do (see v. 9e); *then creation will sing.*

THE YEAR OF HIS GOODNESS

The high point of the section is in verse 11a when David describes the visit of God as the period when He shall have crowned the year of His goodness. Here we have one of the loveliest designations for the kingdom rule of Christ in all of the Old Testament: *the year of His goodness.* As this is Yahweh's royal reign, the verb "to crown" seems particularly apt.[8]

The second colon of verse 11 has another significant image in the words, "Your wagon tracks will trickle luxuriance." Here the picture language of the poet evokes God's riding in a

[8]The NASB margin gives the literal meaning of the Hebrew text we are following here; the NASB text reads, "the year *with* Thy bounty."

heavily-laden farm cart as He traverses the heavens. From this cart of luxuriance there is a trickling down onto the earth that transforms the earth from its present state of groaning and travail to that of release, vitality, life, and beauty.

Verses 12 and 13 grow quite naturally from this central emphasis of verse 11. In this year of God's goodness, luxuriance will trickle on the renovated earth like fat sloshing from a cart. This luxuriance will trickle to the wilderness areas, which will then become pastures. Formerly bare mountains will gird themselves with rejoicing. The meadows will clothe themselves with flocks, and the valleys will envelope themselves with grain.

Kidner speaks of this scene as "the fantasy of hills and fields putting on their finest clothes and making merry together."[9] Our approach is that this is no fantasy, nor is it a seasonal or local scene. Rather, this highly emotive and figurative language speaks pictorially of the glorious future age when God is King, when heaven has come down, when Jesus is on the throne of David.

In the year of God's goodness creation will sing. Look again at the words that close the poem: "They will shout for joy, Yes, they will sing!" (v. 13cd). *At last we have song!* Now we hear the music promised in the superscription. This was the music made mysterious in the promised vow of verse 1. Praise which was silent is now vocal; the vow has been performed, and music now is heard. The antecedents for the words *they* in verse 13c are the pastures and hills of verse 12 and the meadows and valleys of verse 13ab. Creation now cleansed and freed of its curse sings to the glory of God.

In these words we have figurative language, to be sure. But we do not dismiss the words as merely a figure. Figurative language is figurative of something. The figurative language

---

[9]Kidner, *Psalms,* vol. 2, p. 232. His analysis is that "this joy is seasonal and the scene local; but it is no far cry from this to the glimpse in other psalms (e.g. 96; 98) of a final coming of God, and a welcome from the whole creation" (p. 233).

of this Psalm speaks of the reality of the coming kingdom of Jesus Christ. The experience we should all share in anticipation is one of great joy. If hills and valleys, meadows and pastures are to "sing," are not we also to join in the music?

On reflecting on the way this chapter began, it was perhaps a bit too harsh to picture the conductor of the orchestra and choir never giving the downbeat for *any* music. For, whereas the vow of praise is yet to be fulfilled by creation, there are days so beautiful and scenes so splendid that we feel creation is "tuning up." The song may be still ahead, but some vocalizing is heard from time to time to keep us waiting.

At its best, creation today promises something more. In enjoying a particularly lovely spring day, we cannot forget the severe storms of winter. In observing a lushly forested hillside, we are aware of the barren places beyond. In singing of the bounty of our gardens, we cannot ignore the millions who are hungry. The Fall has taken its toll, indeed.

Nature in its beauty today is like an unfulfilled promise. But one day all imperfections will be gone. Then the hills and the pastures, the meadows and the valleys will all be alive with music—music in praise to the Creator who has instituted the year of His goodness. It will be in the year of His goodness that *creation will sing.*

Our song should be in full voice right now!

CHAPTER 14

Psalm 146
While I Live

I'll praise my Maker while I've breath
And when my voice is lost in death,
Praise shall employ my nobler pow'rs.
My days of praise shall ne'er be past,
While life and thought and being last,
Or immortality endures.

—Isaac Watts

Part One of this book concluded with the lovely words of Psalm 146 (see Chapter 7). I wish to conclude the second part of the book in a similar manner by looking a bit more closely at this beautiful poem of confidence in God.

A DETERMINATION TO PRAISE YAHWEH

Psalm 146 may be analyzed as having four movements. The Psalm begins and concludes with imperatives to praise God. Within these commands to praise Him are two movements declaring the reasonableness of the praise of God and the characteristics of the God of praise. The substance and the tone of this Psalm are directly in line with the thesis of this book. Praise *is* a matter of life and breath.

The first movement of Psalm 146 is made of verses 1 to 2, where we see that *the psalmist determines to praise Yahweh as long as he has life.*

(1)   Hallelujah!
       Praise Yahweh, O my soul!

(2)   I am determined to praise Yahweh while I live,
        I am determined to sing to my God while I have
        life.

Psalm 146 is one of the great Hallel Psalms (Pss. 111–118, 136, 146–150). This Psalm is marked off by the Hebrew shout, "Hallelujah!" at the beginning (v. 1a) as well as at the end of the Psalm (v. 10c). As seen in Psalm 113, the word "Hallelujah!" is an imperative to praise God. It is a command to render to Him boastful, excited delight. By form this word would be directed toward the community: "(You) Praise the Lord."

This Psalm then turns the command back to the psalmist himself, as though the command had bounced off of a wall. Rather than merely command others to praise God, the psalmist says that he is to be excited himself in the praise of God. We are reminded of the words of Psalm 103:1,2:

> Bless Yahweh, O my soul;
> And let all that is within me bless His holy name.
> Bless Yahweh, O my soul;
> And forget not all His benefits.

The distinctive of these words in our present passage lies in their statement of *determination*. The psalmist commands his soul, his real self, his life essence—to be excitedly boastful about God. Then he states that he is determined to praise and to sing to Yahweh his God. The determination in the second verse comes from the Hebrew verbal forms (cohortatives of determination).

Praise *should* come naturally, but some Christians never praise God. Praise *should* come regularly, but many believers are only sporadic in their statements of delight in Him. Is not praise another element of our walk for which renewed commitments become necessary?

This Psalm presents a renewed determination to praise Yahweh as long as one has life.

A DELIGHT IN PRAISING YAHWEH

In saying that praise should be a matter of determination and commitment, I do not wish to imply that praise is a difficult or an unpleasant task. The second section of Psalm 146 (vv. 3–6) shows us that *the psalmist delights in praising Yahweh, his only help and hope.* He does this by showing the folly of trusting any alternatives to God, and the contrasting delight of trusting—and praising—the God of reality. In these words the psalmist now turns to the community and begins to give instruction.

> (3) Do not trust in princes,
> In mortal man in whom there is no salvation.
> (4) When their spirit departs, they return to the ground;
> In that very day their plans come to nothing.

In this section the psalmist first *denies that help or hope are to be found in the creature who is mortal and frail.* I do not wish to suggest that the Bible is here teaching that kind of "rugged individualism" in which one claims no need of community or people. But what the psalmist is denying is that *ultimate* solutions may be found in any other than God.

The picture language of these verses emphasizes how frail and limited the creature is. When he dies, any help he might have given passes on with him. Ultimate help must be found only in the Creator. I believe that it is important to see that the ones being contrasted with God are not evil or deficient men. They are termed "princes." Even the best of people, who may render considerable aid and comfort, may not be compared to God. The best of people are frail and mortal; He is the eternal Creator. Mere mortals are not saviors. All men die and are buried (contrast v. 10a) and their plans die with them.

In strong antithetical parallelism to these words of verses 3 and 4 are the words of verses 5 and 6:

> (5) O how happy is he whose help is the God of Jacob,
>   Whose hope is in Yahweh his God,
> (6) The Maker of heaven and earth,
>   The sea and all that is in them,
>   Who keeps faithfulness forever.

Here the psalmist *affirms that all help and hope are found in the Creator who is faithful forever.* In contrast to trusting in man who is mortal and frail, the beatitude of these verses is pronounced on the one who trusts in God who is eternal and almighty. Why ever should one trust in the creature when he might trust in the Creator?

The phrasing of verse 5 affords a splendid opportunity to see the positive results of observing Hebrew parallelism or stereometrics. The first colon speaks of God in the phrase "the God of Jacob." This relates to God's covenantal relationship to the patriarchs. All of the history of God's faithful dealings with His people are enwrapped in this phrase.

When we look to the God of Jacob for our help, we are standing in the tradition of faith that has extended for some four millennia. From the time of the patriarchs to our own day, God has been proven to be faithful to His word, true to His covenant, never veering from His promises. Four thousand years serve as an incredible test of the faithfulness of God. Then when we realize that God has existed for all eternity—never changing—then even the four millennia pale before the witness of His fidelity.

The second part of verse 5 speaks of God in the words "Yahweh his God." Not only is God the faithful Maker of the covenant with His people so very long ago, but He is the present and personal God who relates Himself to each believer. That is, complementing the history of God's dealings with His people is the present relationship He has with each believer.

These two lines of poetry work together to give a most impressive statement of the ultimate resources we have in our God. He is help and hope for His people. All of His history and all of His present relationships buttress these inner-workings. We *delight* to trust and praise this God.

CREATOR OF THE COSMOS

Not only is God faithful forever as the help and hope of the believer, He is also the Creator of the cosmos. The contrast could not be more pronounced than it is between verses 4 and 6. When we read of God that He is "the maker of heaven and earth," we are taken back to Genesis 1:1. The God who created the cosmos is the Protector of His people. The One who has made the heavens and the earth is the help and hope of the trusting believer. How could one ever choose an alternative? He is not mortal and frail; He is the Creator of all that is.

In the next words of verse 6 we read, "the sea and all that is in them." In these words we have first of all an extension of the extent of God's creative activity. He has made the heavens, the earth, and the sea. There is likely a second level of intent in these words. The concept of God's mastery of the sea and its contents is implied in the fact that He has created the sea. While not overt in this Psalm, the Canaanite concept of hostile and malevolent deities of the sea cannot be too far from the poet's thinking. Over all such supposed opponents and forces of disorder, there is Yahweh the Creator in calm control and sure mastery.

The last colon of verse 6 reads, "Who keeps faithfulness forever." These last words are climactic. Some scholars wish to rework the poetry of verse 6 by having this last colon become a parallel to the first part of verse 7. I believe that such an approach misses the climactic element in this last part of the verse. The point seems to be that this God of covenantal bond, of personal relationship, the Creator of all that is, the Master of the sea—*this God* remains faithful in these relationships for all of His eternity. Here is our sure ground for confidence.

We may observe that this quality of faithfulness that God demonstrates, He also delights to find in His people. Of Moses Yahweh spoke, "In all My house he is faithful" (Num. 12:7b). Because Yahweh is keeping faithfulness forever, we are blessed forever who trust in Him.

A BEATITUDE OF PRAISE

We have seen something about who He is. We may now observe what we are who trust in Him. We are "blessed" (v. 5a). Our English word "blessed" may have something of a static sound to it. The original Hebrew term is not static at all, but is pulsing with excitement. This word is an intensive plural and is an exclamatory word: "O the manifold happinesses of. . . ." The Book of Psalms begins with this word (see Ps. 1:1). This word is characteristic of the wisdom writers. In Greek dress this concept is given pride of place in our Lord's "Sermon on the Mount" (see Matt. 5:3–11).

Not only is the word "blessed" to be seen as descriptive of the believer who trusts in Yahweh, but also the implied antonym "cursed" may depict the unbeliever who trusts in a substitute for God (see vv. 3,4). The antithetical parallelism of verses 3 to 4 and 5 to 6 suggest the implied curse in the first section.

The beatitude on trusting in God (see v. 5) forms the heart of this Psalm. Hear again these words. Take the time to read them aloud. These are the most important words in this poem:

O the manifold happiness of the one whose help is in the
God of Jacob,
Whose hope is in Yahweh his God.

There can be no greater blessing than to be related to the God
of creation forever and to have Him as help and hope for all
time. All of His dealings in the past and all of His present
reality unite to encourage us to keep on trusting in His
continuing faithfulness.

A DESCRIPTION OF YAHWEH OF PRAISE

The third movement of Psalm 146 is made of verses 7 to 9.
Here *the psalmist describes the Yahweh of praise, whoever
aids the helpless and the hopeless.*

(7) He acts with justice to the oppressed,
He gives food to the hungry,
Yahweh sets prisoners free.
(8) Yahweh opens the eyes of the blind,
Yahweh raises those who are bowed down,
Yahweh loves the righteous.
(9) Yahweh watches over aliens.
Orphan and widow He sustains,
But the way of the wicked He twists.

In these three verses of tricola, we have eight elements that
are in synonymous parallelism, with the ninth in antithetical
relationship to the first eight. We are reminded in the first
eight elements that *our God characteristically aids the helpless and the weak.* These words flesh out the central declaration of the Psalm, found in verses 5 and 6. Our help and hope
may be in Him (v. 5), because He guards faithfulness forever
(v. 6). This truth is consequent with His character; it is
consistent with His name.

The characteristic element of verses 7–9b is seen in the

types of verbs used in the original text. Most of these verbs are Hebrew participles. These are the verbs: "He acts," "He gives," "He sets free" [v. 7], "He opens eyes," "He raises up," "He loves" [v. 8], "He watches over" [v. 9a]. These participles express durative, continuous action. These activities of God are not simply to be seen from time to time; they are regularly to be expected as the outflow of grace and love from our caring God. The verb in verse 8b ("He raises up") is an habitual imperfect, which speaks of repetitive action. Yahweh *characteristically* meets the needs of His people.

The importance of these assertions cannot be overstressed. When we speak of the actions of God as characteristic, we are drawing a contrast to pagan deities who were notoriously fickle and unpredictable. The gods of the imagination are motivated by caprice, not character. The deities of paganism are prompted by whim, not wisdom. For example, in the Babylonian account of the Flood, the reason given for the destruction of mankind was that mankind's ruckus disturbed the gods in their midday naps. But in bringing devastation on all mankind these whimsical deities forgot that they were cutting off their complete food supply. The Babylonian counterpart to Noah offered sacrifices to the gods after leaving his ark. The ancient Mesopotamian record then describes the hungry gods descending on the sacrifice like flies.

Against all of the deities of the imagination whose characters are unworthy of devotion, there stands the biblical testimony that the God of reality acts with characteristic deeds to meet the needs of His people.

The nouns of verses 7 to 9 are mostly descriptive of the helpless and the hopeless. Observe these words again and listen to their dirge: "the oppressed," "the hungry," "the prisoners" (v. 7), "the blind," "the bowed down" (v. 8ab), "the alien," "the orphan and widow" (v. 9ab). Each of these terms is descriptive of that kind of person who cannot help himself and who has no hope in himself.

The one phrase in this list that is more positive is "the righteous" (v. 8c). Yet often in the Book of Psalms "the righteous" are described as under affliction, receiving abuse, or being despised. In Psalm 14:4 God's people are devoured as one might eat bread. In Psalm 12:1 help seems to have ceased for the pious. These and other such factors are what led to the Psalms of lament. In Psalm 146 "the righteous" are seen among those who are helpless and hopeless in themselves. But "the righteous" are also those who have found their help and hope in the ever-faithful God of Israel.

We should be impressed with the repeated use of the name of God in this section. The name "Yahweh" is found five times as the first member of each colon in verses 7c–9a. He is the unnamed subject of the first two cola (7a, 7b) and the last two (9b, 9c). The characteristic blessings of God proceed from the character that is resplendent in His great name.

Not only does this section of the Psalm speak of the characteristic actions of Yahweh in bringing comfort to the weak (vv. 7a–9b). The poem also affirms that *He characteristically confounds the wicked* (v. 9c). With another habitual imperfect verbal form, the psalmist describes God as thwarting or twisting the way of the wicked. "The wicked" would be that person who refuses to find in Yahweh his or her source of help and hope. This is the antonym of "the righteous" of verse 8c.

Psalm 146 began with the determination of the psalmist to praise Yahweh who is ever faithful (vv. 1,2). Then it moved to the delight of the psalmist in praising Yahweh, our only help and hope (vv. 3–6). Next we saw a description of the Yahweh of praise, who ever aids the helpless and the hopeless (vv. 7–9). We are now prepared for the last movement of the Psalm.

A DEMAND FOR THE PRAISE OF YAHWEH

The last verse of Psalm 146 presents the concluding thought of the passage as *the psalmist demands the praise of Yahweh, who reigns for all time.*

(10) Yahweh reigns forever;
Your God, O Zion, for generation after generation.
Hallelujah!

In these last words we observe that the reign of God is presently active. The verb "to reign" should be in the present tense ("reigns," as above and in the NIV), and not in the future ("will reign," as in the NASB). This verb is also an habitual imperfect. He reigns now and will reign forever. Not only does He presently reign, but He specifically reigns *for the good of His own*. Such is the direction of the words, "Your God, O Zion." That he reigns forever is a maxim of theology. That He reigns forever for my good is an expression of my relationship to the King of glory.

His reign for my good elicits the final command: "Hallelujah!—Be excitedly boastful about Yahweh!"

THE FRUIT OF PRAISE

Among the many manuscripts found in the caves of Qumran there were some scrolls that were composed by the people of the Dead Sea sect. One of the most important of these has been entitled by modern writers "the Manual of Discipline." This text describes the rules for the community along with their ideals, their basic theology, and their purposes as a sect. Within this document there are many allusions to the Old Testament and many concepts that grow directly out of the Hebrew Scriptures.

The Manual of Discipline concludes with a splendid Psalm that shows many of the elements that we have seen in our study of the biblical Psalms. One section seems particularly appropriate to our reading of Psalm 146. These are the words from this "new" Psalm from Qumran:

As long as I exist a decree engraved shall be on my tongue
For fruit of praise and for a gift of my lips.

PRAISE! A MATTER OF LIFE AND BREATH

I will sing with knowledge,
And all my music shall be for the glory of God;
My lyre and harp shall be for His holy fixed order,
And the flute of my lips I will raise
In His just circle.[1]

Here we have words that grow out of Psalm 146 and other similar poems in the Bible. The normal setting for praise is in the circle of the just ones, the community of the redeemed. Praise is the gift of the lips. Praise is for the glory of God. Praise is to be done with knowledge. Praise is to be done with determination. *By a life of praise we respond to our always faithful God.*

The biblical psalmist says, "I am determined to praise Yahweh while I live" (Ps. 146:2). The later Jewish poet echoes, "As long as I exist a decree engraved shall be on my tongue/for the fruit of praise and for a gift of my lips."

May all who read these words make a similar determination, borne by the Spirit of God. May we join that happy people who have, as it were, the decree to praise God engraved on their very tongue. God desires the fruit of praise. He delights in the gift of the lips.

[1]From the *Manual of Discipline,* trans. Millar Burrows, *The Dead Sea Scrolls,* reprint ed. (Grand Rapids: Baker, 1978), p. 385.

CHAPTER 15

Rachel—God's Lamb

Oh heaven! What a moment is this!
Oh, joy inexpressibly sweet!
Righteous is Thy judgment, oh God,
Thou triest us, Thou doest not forsake us.

—Joseph von Sonnleithner/
Ludwig von Beethoven,
Fidelio

The preceding chapters were written in Manila during my sabbatical as a guest professor at the Asian Theological Seminary. In these chapters I attempted to express what I believe to be the major teaching of the Book of Psalms concerning the life of praise.

Shortly after our return to the States in mid-December 1978, our family faced a crisis that put the issues of this book to a new and difficult test. This present chapter details how God allowed us to experience the depths, and from the depths—by His grace—to continue to praise His name.

On Thursday morning, March 8, 1979, our comfortable world began to crumble. Yet, as I look back on that day I realize that it really began with many promises. We were still in the process of readjustment to our life back in Oregon. The winter quarter at the Seminary was drawing to an uncommonly quick close, and I still had much to do.

Meanwhile, back at the ranch, our little farmlet was yearning for spring after a winter of record ice and cold. Our two goat does were due to kid in a couple of weeks, our garden was planned on paper, and I was ready to order some day-old chicks.

So the day really began flushed with promise. However, my wife, Beverly, and our twenty-one-month-old Rachel drove in with me that morning, as Beverly wanted to take the baby to our pediatrician. Rachel had been having one infection after another since our return from Asia. The night before she had not slept at all. She was feverish and had eruptions on her skin known as *petechiae,* small bleeding points—an indicator of serious illness.

When I came to my office after my morning class I was met by Beverly. She told me that we would have to take Rachel directly to the hospital for some tests. The pediatrician was most concerned about her condition. He suspected a serious disease (perhaps spinal meningitis) or some major problem in Rachel's ability to fight infection. We had been thinking that because of the aftereffects of a serious infection in Taiwan that Rachel was just more susceptible to infection. Our doctor believed the problem was more serious than that. I cancelled my afternoon class. Cracks were beginning to appear in our comfortable world.

By the end of the day the cracks had led to crumbling. I never mailed the order for the chicks. We stopped bantering about for names for our anticipated goat kids. The garden was delayed. And grading papers—that too was given a further setback. By evening it was believed highly likely that Rachel was suffering from leukemia, a diagnosis that was to be confirmed on the next day. Our pediatrician was visibly shaken. We met the specialist in pediatric hematology who confronted us with the initial findings and told us of plans to transfer Rachel to the university hospital the next morning.

Leukemia! This is one of those dread-words that one reads about in news accounts concerning others. In fact, earlier that week we had read of parents who had decided to have their child with this disease treated in Mexico rather than in their eastern city. But this time it was not they, but *we*. Beverly is a pediatric nurse, and she determined to stay in the hospital room with Rachel, while I was to go home to tell the rest of our children the hard news.

It had been a beautiful early spring day in Portland. The air was fresh; the sky clear. But on the drive home I still had trouble seeing the highway. As I drove on the interstate I wept aloud in the privacy of the car. Then the words, "Why, Lord?" came to mind. But as I drove I resisted these words and their implications.

For years I have worked in, and lived in, the Psalms of Israel. I know about the Psalms of lament in which God is challenged and questioned by the believer under pressure. But that condition of lament cannot be permitted to last, or one's joy in the Lord will be replaced by bitterness, one's praise of God will be silenced, and one's very life will lose much of its meaning.

For these reasons, even as tears chased each other down my cheeks, I determined not to live in the "Why, Lord?" syndrome. These words seemed inappropriate to me for three reasons. First, they might betray an assumption that life is always rational, that reasons will always be apparent. Yet we learn from the Book of Ecclesiastes that often life is an enigma. Ecclesiastes 3:11, for example, declares the contrasting truths that God does all things beautifully, but He may also keep His purposes hidden from His people. There are some puzzles in our living for which answers are not forthcoming.

A second reason for resisting the common complaint, "Why, Lord?" is that these words suggest an implied arrogance that God (who is Master and Lord!) owes His people explanations for His deeds and for those things He allows. Pots are not made to challenge the Potter.

A third reason that the lament seemed inappropriate lies in the fact that if these words are spoken too angrily, they may border on blasphemy.

So before I left the interstate for the narrower roads leading to our home, I decided to ask another question: "What now, Lord?" That is, given the grim spectre of catastrophic illness in our little daughter, how may we now live the life of praise? Further, in this restated question, I wished to magnify the concept of God as *Lord*, the Sovereign, the Suzerain of my life. On that long road home I renewed my determination to praise God while I have life.

When I arrived, our little boy Bruce was already asleep. But Laureen and Craig and my mother were anxious to hear the news from the hospital. We began reading articles on leukemia in our encyclopedias and in some medical dictionaries. Words seared across our eyes saying "nearly always fatal." Craig broke down. "Then she's going to die," he cried. I tried to comfort him and myself with the words, "Not necessarily. Our God is still *Lord*." Then we all prayed, but we slept little that night.

THE LIFE IS IN THE BLOOD

On Friday, March 9, we entered a whole new world of medical terms and procedures. Rachel was diagnosed as having *acute lymphoblastic leukemia* (abbreviated A.L.L.) in an advanced stage. This cancer of the blood manifests itself in several ways. Malignant blood cells (called *blast* cells) develop in the bone marrow, crowding out normally developing blood cells.

These immature white cells divide too early and are of no value to the blood. The consequent loss of healthy red blood cells leaves the patient with severe anemia. This may result in a loss of the will to live. The loss of the normal white blood cells leaves the patient defenseless against infection and severely hampered in bodily healing. The loss of the platelets leaves the patient open to bruising and bleeding. A common sign of this last factor is the appearance of *petechiae,* the small bleeding points near the surface of the skin that we had observed on Rachel's body the day before.

"The life is in the blood." This Old Testament affirmation (see Lev. 17:11,14) has become extraordinarily more meaningful to us in these days. Without blood, without sufficient healthy blood, one simply cannot live.

After a lengthy, traumatic day of medical procedures and diagnostic tests done for Rachel, the doctors then met with Beverly and me to explain our new realities. We were encouraged to learn that the treatment of this disease had advanced considerably in the last five years. There is still no cure for this type of leukemia, but there is a course of treatment that usually brings about remission in from two to four weeks. The word "remission" is used to describe a patient in whom the disease is no longer detected. Because there may be latent cancer cells hiding in the body, tests need to be made periodically to determine if the patient is still in remission.

The type of treatment our daughter was to have was quite complex—the result of a great deal of experimentation over the last several years. She was to begin intensive chemotherapy treatment in a program (or protocol) that would last for six weeks. This would be augmented by antibiotic therapy because of the high levels of infection that she had, as well as blood therapy because of her own depleted resources. Finally, there would be a two week regimen of central nervous system radiation therapy to insure the destruction of remaining malignant cells.

The maintenance chemotherapy might be prescribed for three more years, with periodic "pulse" phases of intensive treatment lasting for about one month. Such went the explanation of our physicians. They instilled in us a cautious optimism, an optimism guarded with the sobering reality that our daughter was in critical condition. We were given books to read, charts to study, and a new vocabulary to explore. This is not to mention new emotions and pains.

229

A DETERMINATION TO PRAISE THE LORD

Throughout that first week of hospitalization, Beverly and I determined to praise God, whatever would be the course of His present action. We wanted our little girl to live—of course! But whether she would live or die, we wanted most of all to be parents who would be learning new ways to give praise to God's name.

In this determination to give praise to God, we were greatly encouraged by the words of Psalm 146 (see Chapter 14). This Psalm declares joyfully the determination of the hurting believer to praise God who is ever faithful. I believe that God led me into a new study of that Psalm at a time when it would be unforgettable.

In the words of Psalm 146, we were determined that so long as we have life we will praise God. There did not seem to be any reason to wallow in our distress. Rather, from the depths we wished to honor the Lord. We recounted the numerous times over the past several months that God had blessed us in extraordinary ways. We reminded each other that the God we had trusted in the past was still worthy of our trust.

OUR HELP AND HOPE

Psalm 146:3,4 speaks of the folly of placing ultimate hope in any one less than our great God. In balance with these words, denying the creature as the object of hope or the ultimate source of help, I wish to assert how *much* help and hope we did receive from many dear people.

We were encouraged immensely by the greatly supportive medical personnel at the hospital. Doctors and nurses were so caring and so giving we shall always remember them with love. What special people God gave us in those dark days. Rachel was not a "case" to them in our perception. She was a hurting little girl that they ministered to as an individual. In addition to those people who were daily visible, there were many people in the background to whom we owe much, but whom we never met. These would be lab technicians, Red Cross personnel, and many others.

We also found tremendous encouragement from the people of our local church. Our pastor and Christian friends showed in many ways their love for us and their concern for Rachel. The people in our congregation brought food to us once a week so that Beverly would be able to stay in the hospital without the worry of preparing meals. The meals presented by the ladies of our church were placed in the freezer each week. All we had to do was heat them.

These caring Christians prayed for us, gave us money, donated blood for us, and aided us in many other ways. One indelible impression from our whole experience has been the renewed sense of community we felt within our home church. (I frankly do not know how a non-Christian family can cope with catastrophic illness—particularly of children—lacking the much needed support of a caring Christian community. We observed one such family in great distress, but with no comfort, during those days.)

But our ultimate help and hope was not in these people, as good and noble as they are. For Psalm 146 states clearly that even princes would not suffice for ultimate hope. That is a reminder that the genuinely happy person is the one who finds help and hope in Yahweh (v. 5). Even our good friends and our caring doctors cannot suffice for ultimate hope and help. They are limited by their own frailty and mortality, but God is blessed forever as the Creator and Sustainer of the universe.

How truly happy is the one whose help is the God of Jacob,
Whose hope is in Yahweh his God (Ps. 146:5).

Day after day we were strengthened by words such as these as Rachel continued to suffer and failed to respond to treatment. When she was released from the hospital, it was only briefly. New infections caused lengthened and repeated stays. The first two weeks passed, and there was no remission. Instead, Rachel was still quite ill and in the hospital. When three weeks had gone by, she seemed to be worse rather than improved.

At the end of the four weeks that should have brought the good news of her remission, she was in fact more seriously ill. In addition to a major infection in her rectum that caused great pain and which was symptomatic of the latter stages of the disease, there was a new site of virulent infection near her right knee. Our doctors told us that this was most serious indeed. Not only had Rachel not responded to chemotherapy, but she had a major new infection in the face of almost constant antibiotics.

Beverly stayed with Rachel night and day, week after week. She was both mother and nurse to her. I would come to the hospital after classes to visit both of them. I found that Rachel seemed to like to have me hold her hand. She was not yet speaking—a problem that compounded our grief as we could not know how much she understood of her illness. Our time in the Orient had come just as she was beginning to speak. Then, with the new babel of tongues about her, the rules of language seemed changed, and she had given up trying for a while. With the illness she was not up to trying anything.

Sometimes I would sing children's hymns to her, softly, such as "Jesus Loves Me." At the words, "they are weak," I would occasionally falter. Rachel had always been very affectionate and full of smiles and laughter. For weeks she had not smiled. Worse, she hurt too badly to want to be held or cuddled. As the disease built up pressure within the bone marrow, Rachel experienced bone pain. She could not bear to have us pick her up from her bed. It simply hurt too much.

She mourned the loss of her hair much more than we might have thought for one so very young. Daily Bev would take tape and wipe off large gobs of hair from the sheets and pillows as it would come out in clumps from the side effects of the toxic drugs. It was a very sad day when Beverly had to put the last of the barrettes away in a drawer. There was not enough hair to hold them. Taping them on did not work either. During those days, Rachel liked to play with Beverly's hair as a substitute for her own.

One of the saddest days came when the doctors decided that Rachel could not have any food or liquids by mouth for a period of time—which lasted a couple of days. The one source of comfort Rachel had seemed to cling to was her bottle. Now even that was gone.

One of our close Christian friends remarked on this directive that there are times in our lives when God must treat us in a similar way. There are times when God takes away things that we are used to and which we expect. He does not do this to hurt us, no more than the doctors had taken away Rachel's bottle for her hurt. For reasons known only to Himself, He does these things for our good. But like an uncomprehending infant, we still cry for our bottle and cannot understand why the rules have been changed.

But we kept coming back to the words of the Psalms, and particularly to the words of Psalm 146:5:

> How truly happy is the one whose help is the God of Jacob,
> Whose hope is in Yahweh his God.

We would not say "Why, Lord?" We continued to ask, "What next, Lord?" We determined to praise Him whatever might come.

WHO AIDS THE HELPLESS AND THE HOPELESS

At the end of five weeks we faced the most distressing news of all. In addition to the fact that Rachel was still not in remission (something we expected between two to four weeks), her infections continued to cause considerable discomfort. Weeks of constant antibiotics had not controlled these. Her leg wound was more seriously inflamed, and her rectum was causing her great pain.

The worst news was that the blood tests that day showed new blast cells in her system. These new malignant cells suggested that the chemotherapy was failing.

On Thursday, April 12, two doctors sat in our room and shared their sad conclusions. The course of treatment designed to bring induction into remission had only one week to go. They would see the same treatment through that week. But since Rachel had not responded with eighty percent of the treatment completed, our doctor believed that it was quite unlikely that she would do much differently on receiving the remaining twenty percent. The major question we would have to face in a week's time was how much longer we could perpetuate her suffering before facing a terminal situation.

This was a day of renewed weeping. All of the emotions of the previous five weeks came to a head. Not only were we weeping, but so were others. On Saturday our pediatrician came for a visit. He sat down after looking at Rachel's deteriorating condition. Tears came down his cheeks as they did ours.

But as we wept, we also kept trusting in God. *Whom else is there to trust?* And we kept looking for opportunities to magnify the name of God. Beverly was able to minister in the lives of several hospital personnel, sharing her trust in the God who is ever faithful.

We prayed that Rachel would live. But if she were to die, we prayed that we would honor Him out of our distress. Finding ourselves to be helpless and hopeless apart from Him, we

234

renewed our dedication as a family to trust in His perfect character. We do not understand why children suffer; we do know God's mercy. We do not understand why children die; we do know God's love. We did not understand why Rachel was still critical; we did—and do—know God's character.

We know that it is characteristic of God to help those who cannot help themselves. This is the clear teaching of verses 7 through 9 of Psalm 146. Our prayer was that He would magnify Himself in our midst by bringing our little girl into remission *in the face* of the seemingly hopeless situation.

But we did not know if God would grant her healing. For that reason our family talked about funeral plans for her. We knew how badly we felt at the prospect of her death. We assumed we would feel worse when her death was a fact. So we desired to prepare for her funeral before the fact, so that we would be able to plan well for God's glory and our comfort.

I remember one night talking to Rachel and praying to God in her room. I looked again at her expressive eyes, now so filled with pain. I saw again the brown fleck in one of her hazel eyes. I wondered, might it be that this distinctive coloration of her eyes will be the means by which I will recognize her in heaven? We knew, of course, that should she die, God in His great mercy would take her to be with the Lord Jesus in heaven. There she would have no more pain. There disease would never again tear out her joy. When we wept, it was for ourselves.

I did tell some of my friends at school that Friday, April 12, that I would appreciate prayer for Rachel that she might improve sufficiently to be released from the hospital for a period of time that we might have her at home with us for some days. At the same time, we kept prayers assaulting the heavens based on the character of God and His characteristic help to those without hope. We never doubted God's ability to raise Rachel from her illness. We prayed—and many joined us—that He would do so.

THE DELIGHT OF PRAISING GOD

In the sixth—and determinative—week there was some change indicated on Wednesday. On that day Rachel's blood tests showed an improvement in the white blood cell count. This was something unexpected, as there had been several days since her last transfusion of packed white cells. One doctor, not wishing to raise our hopes only to have them dashed again, said that there might have been an error made in the count. All would be made clear on Friday, however, as then another bone marrow test would be made. Because of the reports of the last few weeks, the doctors were expecting the worst: a recurrence of packed blast cells.

On Friday morning, April 20, I was in my office at the seminary. We were told that the test results would likely come after lunch. I decided to try to teach my eleven o'clock class, and then I planned to go to the hospital to meet with Beverly and the doctors.

I knew that there was a possibility that the results would be known earlier than lunch time, so I stayed in my office during the chapel time just in case Beverly might phone. At 10:33 A.M. Bev did phone. She said that one of the doctors attending Rachel had just come into her room, bursting with a smile and saying, "I have the best possible news: Rachel is in remission!"

Remission! A word that was as beautiful as *leukemia* was ugly. Remission—after all of those weeks. Remission—when it seemed that drugs and treatments had failed.

Words take on unique beauty in contexts of despair. To a starving Cambodian, what word is more beautiful than *rice*? To a prisoner-of-war, what word is more desired than *release*? To the parents of a child believed to be dying of cancer, what word can be more lovely than *remission*? Only one word, I suppose: the name of God, the eternal Yahweh, who brought it about!

The doctor added that there was no mistake. She had

checked the results herself. "I know many people have been praying for you. It seems their prayers have been answered." Indeed! How we praise Your name, our great God!

Imagine our joy! We felt a bit what the disciples must have experienced when they knew our Lord had burst forth from the grave. We shared the joy of the woman of Zerephath when Elijah bore her son from his upper room and said, "See, your son is alive!" (1 Kin. 17:23). We thought we were losing Rachel to death, but now we had her back! Our God, who is ever faithful, had demonstrated one more time how He characteristically aids the helpless and the hopeless. The Psalms of praise *must* be sung, and the words of delight *must* be said. He is good and He is faithful. He has met our needs.

After the telephone call I made my way over to the chapel, which was still in session. At the end of the special lecture by a guest speaker, I was given an opportunity by our president to share with the seminary family our great news of God's goodness. Praise has to be done in the community. Then all may rejoice.

The words of Humperdinck's closing couplet to *Hansel and Gretel* came back again with a new intensity:

> When our need is at its greatest,
> God the Lord stretches out to us His hand!

It is characteristic of God to stretch forth His gracious hand at the moment of deep need. Glory then must come to Himself.

We appreciate our physicians and nurses. We are glad for the facility of the university hospital and our proximity to it. We have benefited from technology, research, treatments, drugs, and radiation therapy. Many people that we may never know worked behind the scenes in labs and in clinics on our behalf. Yet we know that *ultimately all healing is from God.*

God may heal using the means of modern medicine and the skills of caring physicians. He may also heal by using extraordinary means when medical procedures fail or are insufficient. In any and in every case, praise is due His name.

We do not know what the future holds for our daughter Rachel; we do know our God. We do not know how long she shall live; we do know that He reigns forever for our good. We shall live with her disease "one day at a time," as we were encouraged to do in the book on leukemia given us by our doctors.

But we shall also praise God one day at a time while we live and have our being.

The name *Rachel* is a Hebrew word meaning "ewe-lamb." Rachel is God's little lamb.

By His great grace, she is our lamb as well.

CHAPTER 16

Coda
The Breath of Life

All that hath life and breath,
Come now with praises before Him!

—Joachim Neander

Praise is the natural effulgence, the radiant splendor, of the believer in the God of reality. One who is rightly related to the Lord of glory, and who thinks rightly of that relationship, cannot but adore Him with all that is within. The eternal, triune God has acted in such knowledge, wisdom, compassion, mercy, holiness, justice, righteousness, grace, and love to His own that we, the objects of these excellencies, *must* respond to Him in great praise.

In his letter to the Ephesians the apostle Paul begins his first chapter by describing the acts of the great Yahweh for His people in the splendors of His triunity. As Paul concludes each section of this triptych of theology, he naturally and exuberantly interjects words of praise. The work of the Father for us is "to the praise of the glory of His grace" (Eph. 1:6a). The work of the Son for us is "to the praise of His glory" (v. 12). The work of the Spirit for us is "to the praise of His glory" (v. 14).

The natural and spontaneous joy in the Lord of the new Christian is in full accord with the great theological doxologies of the apostle Paul in this majestic text. How very sad when any believer loses the initial joyful response to God somewhat later in his or her walk. To the extent that praise is dulled, genuine life diminishes. As Westermann concluded, so must we: "There cannot be such a thing as true life without praise."[1]

It is my keen desire that these studies will have brought to you a renewed sense of joy in the Scriptures. To bring this response it was necessary to explore some of the elements that make the Psalms the great literature that they are. It is my hope that in these pages you have learned *to feel with* the Psalms, *to share in* the songs, and *to participate in* these expressions of worship in genuine praise to God.

A major and necessary thrust of this book has been in the nature of the praise of God. Praise has been defined as a public and vocal act of genuine delight in the person and actions of God. As one reflects on the love of the Father, the wonder of Jesus, the presence of the Spirit—praise is a necessary outflow. Praise is excited boasting in the wonder of knowing God. This boasting in God is a natural response to Him. Praise is an *active* expression. It is neither passive nor an escape. It is also God's intention for our lives.

IN SPIRIT AND IN TRUTH

When we think of the term "worship" we sometimes find our thoughts to be somewhat muddled. There are those who wish to worship God out in the woods; others think only of worship in the buildings of the church. The word "worship" may in fact relate to private adoration of God as well as to the public declaration. An individual *may* worship God in the silence of the forest or in the solitude of his "closet." When worship of God is done by the individual, it is usually contemplative and meditative.

But worship usually relates to the community as they magnify the name of God in concert. As one hymnal puts it,

[1]Westermann, *Praise of God,* p. 159.

"When done in congregations, worship is celebrative, as the congregation rehearses, relives, and rejoices in its history as the People of God.[2]

The Psalms would suggest that our patterns of congregational worship may not be all that they should be. Many churches pride themselves on having very little that is formal or liturgical. In doing so, these churches may suffer a lack of dignity, of reverence, of reflecting on the awesomeness of God—and particularly a loss in the opportunity for the members of the congregation to join together in the praise of God.

Similarly, those churches who have treasured the liturgical formulas common to much of the church in its history and in its worldwide expansion may sometimes suffer a lack of spontaneity, of joy, of excitement in adoring the acts of God.

I would suggest that the Psalms give us ample reason for *both* liturgy *and* spontaneity in our worship services. The very *formal nature* of the Psalms would argue for liturgy, for shape and direction to the church at worship. But the *call* of the Psalms is for excitement, for spontaneity, for delight in God and in His deeds today.

As in all things, the hardest element in worship is to achieve a balance of these two factors. Order and structure are not barriers to praise; they are supports of praise, if within the order and structure there are opportunities for freedom and rejoicing.

Jesus called us to worship God "in spirit and in truth" (John 4:23). The Psalms present the substance and the content of that worship.

BOASTING IN HIM

Jeremiah spoke of praise in words that are clear and memorable. Our boasting is not to be in our own excellence,

[2]*The Covenant Hymnal* (Chicago: Covenant, 1973), p. 660.

worth, or ability, but in our relationship with the eternal
Yahweh. These are Jeremiah's words expressing the delight
of God:

> Thus says Yahweh,
> "Let not a wise man boast of his wisdom,
> And let not the mighty man boast of his might,
> Let not a rich man boast of his riches;
> But let him who boasts boast of this,
> That he understands and knows Me,
> That I am Yahweh who exercises loyal love,
> justice, and righteousness on earth;
> For I delight in these things"
> —the solemn utterance of Yahweh (Jer. 9:23,24).

In boasting we do not sin when our boast is in the character
and work of our incomparable God. Moreover, praise is the
great privilege of the life and breath of faith.

EVEN THOSE WHO STUMBLE

Among the many biblical passages found in the caves near
the Dead Sea in the region of Qumran there were also many
nonbiblical portions. One poem that was found in Cave 11 is a
delightful psalm that one editor has termed, "A Plea for
Deliverance." This psalm is not part of the collection in our
Bible, but it breathes much of the spirit of the canonical
hymns. The poem begins with these words:

> Surely a maggot cannot praise You,
> Nor may a grave worm recount Your loyal love.
> But the living can praise You,
> Even those who stumble can laud You.[3]

[3] 11 QPs*a*, col. xix, "Plea for Deliverance," found in J.A. Sanders, *The
Psalms Scroll of Qumran Cave 11,* Discoveries in the Judaean Desert of
Jordan series, vol. 4 (Oxford: Clarendon, 1965), pp. 76–77.

Praise has its forum in life, not in death. Praise is done in the community, not in the grave. Those insects that eat away on dead things are not among the creatures who give praise to God.

But we who are alive may praise Him. We who are alive *must* praise Him. Even those of us who stumble can do one thing right: We may laud the God of glory.

Almost eighty years ago Professor Richard G. Moulton said that almost everything possible has been done with the Bible. It has been analyzed, commented upon, translated, revised, quarreled over, discussed, debated, divided, epitomized, extracted, and the like. Then he said, "There is yet one thing left to do with the Bible: simply to read it.[4]

So it is with the praise of God. The one thing left for us to do is *to do it.*

Praise *is* a matter of life and breath. Won't you join me in a renewed commitment to a life of praising God? A life lived without the praise of God is not really a life worth living. We were created, purposed, redeemed, and blessed "to the praise of His glory." Our chief end as Spirit-led believers in the Lord Jesus Christ is to glorify God and to enjoy Him forever. It is only by a life of praise that we may respond properly to our always faithful God.

Hallelujah!
Praise Yahweh, O *my* soul!
(Ps. 146:1)

---

[4]*A Short Introduction to the Literature of the Bible,* (1901), pp. iii-iv; quoted by William Canton, *The Bible and the Anglo-Saxon People* (London: J.M. Dent & Sons, 1914), p. 279.

SELECTED BIBLIOGRAPHY

Alden, Robert. *Psalms*. 3 vols. Everyman's Bible Commentary series. Chicago: Moody, 1974–77. Brief introductions to the Psalms by the professor of Old Testament at Denver Seminary: especially helpful on structure.

Alexander, Joseph Addison. *The Psalms: Translated and Explained*. Reprint ed. Grand Rapids: Baker, 1975. First published in 1850, this remains a classic commentary.

Barth, Christoph F. *Introduction to the Psalms*. Trans. R. A. Wilson. New York: Charles Scribner's Sons, 1966. This is a good complement to Westermann (below).

Dahood, Mitchell. *Psalms: Introduction, Translation, and Notes*. Anchor Bible series. 3 vols. Garden City, New York: Doubleday, 1966–70. This is the most revolutionary commentary on the Psalms in the history of hymnic research; however, it is difficult for the reader to evaluate.

Kidner, Derek. *Psalms: An Introduction and Commentary*. 2 vols. Downers Grove, Ill.: Inter-Varsity, 1973–75. Brief but very satisfying studies by a fine scholar.

Leupold, H. C. *Exposition of the Psalms*. Grand Rapids: Baker, 1970. A worthy commentary by a leading Lutheran scholar.

Lewis, C. S. *Reflections on the Psalms*. New York: Harcourt, Brace, and World, 1958. One's sensitivity to the literature of the Psalms will be greatly enhanced by the reading of this book.

Perowne, J. J. Stewart. *The Book of Psalms.* 2 vols. Reprint ed. Grand Rapids: Zondervan, 1966. The reviewer's choice among older commentaries; excels in outlines.

Sabourin, Leopold. *The Psalms—Their Origin and Meaning.* Enlarged ed. Staten Island, N. Y.: Alba House, 1974. This volume is particularly helpful as a summary of recent research on the Psalms.

Spurgeon, Charles Haddon. *The Treasury of David.* 5 vols. Reprint ed. Grand Rapids: Eerdmans, n.d. This set is available in several editions. It is outstanding in devotional thought from the English Puritans but is weak in terms of exegesis.

Waltke, Bruce K. "Commentary on the Psalms." *The Expositor's Bible Commentary,* Ed. Frank E. Gaebelein. Grand Rapids: Zondervan, forthcoming. A long anticipated commentary by a master teacher and scholar.

Westermann, Claus. *The Praise of God in the Psalms.* Trans. Keith R. Crim. Richmond, Va.: John Knox, 1965. This volume has been used repeatedly in the present work. A new book by Westermann, *The Psalms* (Minneapolis: Augsburg, 1980), was received too late for use in this present study.